- Da... ...ve
  pla... ...ly
  by...

- Dav... ...he
  gar... ...a
  cou...

- Pau... ...gic
  wa... ...at
  clea... ...ke
  Loo... ..."

- Dar... ...ts
  bor... ...se
  incr... ...k-
  ing, ...
  guy...

- Lar... ...le
  and ... ...he
  leag...

- **Magic Johnson on Larry Bird:** "In the beginning, there
  definitely was rivalry. But it's no personal battle, me
  against him. He's the best, so you've got to bring your
  best. The boy is bad."

MITCHELL KRUGEL

A 2M COMMUNICATIONS LTD. PRODUCTION

ST. MARTIN'S PRESS/NEW YORK

MAGIC AND THE BIRD

Copyright © 1989 by Mitchell Krugel and 2M Communications Ltd.

Photo research by Amanda Rubin.
Cover photographs courtesy Focus on Sports.

ISBN: 0-312-91725-2   Can. ISBN: 0-312-91726-0

Printed in the United States of America

First St. Martin's Press mass market edition/October 1989

10 9 8 7 6 5 4 3 2 1

1

Cheers to Magic and the Bird

THE HEAT WAS SO THICK IT WAS ALMOST VISIBLE, WHICH made even this simple saunter down Causeway Street enough to work up a midgame sweat. As the two men staggered past the old North Station, the evening events became overwhelmed by the temperature. "Damn, Lou, it's hot," said the man wearing his omnipresent Wayfarer sunglasses even though it well past 11 P.M. "I need a drink." So off the two best of friends went, each clad in a fluorescent flowered shirt, to find one of the city's finest taverns.

Lou picked the first place he saw, and Jack followed him down the stairs into what seemed like one of Boston's typical watering holes. But over at the corner of the bar sat one of the house regulars, smoking a big cigar. In this town and in this place, that could only mean that the Celtics had won again, and as Jack looked at this hefty man, he knew he was seeing someone familiar. Could it really be that man—Red Auerbach himself—sitting right there drinking a beer?

"Yeah, how about those Celtics," roared the big man. "Aren't they something, Cliffee? One more victory, the NBA championship, and I won't have to worry about keeping myself to just six beers a day until training camp next season."

"Well, Nahmie," Cliff interrupted, "what you're talking about there is simply the greatest combination of the finest abilities to play the game blended together to form the *crème de la crème* of the league. You got your two great big men, your great guards, your basic great coaching, and Larry Bird."

"Yeah, how about Larry Bird," Norm said with a laugh. "Hey Sammie, how about a round of drinks on the house to toast Larry Bird?"

"Why not," answered Sam. "I remember when someone bought a round of drinks to toast me."

"For what?" jibed the barmaid, "Leaving?"

"Yeah," Sam charged back cleverly. "Well, the only way someone would buy a round of drinks for you is if the place was empty."

"Yeah, how about Larry Bird," Norm said with another laugh.

By now Jack and Lou had heard enough without having a drink. So Jack called the waitress over, and inquired about placing an order. "Honey, bring us a couple of California Coolers," he said as he threw a $100 bill on the table, "and buy those gentlemen whatever they're drinking. Tell them it's compliments of Magic Johnson."

"Hey friend," Normie said as he pointed his finger. "There's no need to compliment Magic Johnson. Not here anyway. In this town, you're a Bird fan and a Bud man or you're nothing. We don't need to wear sunglasses in the middle of the night, either. Who are you supposed to be anyway, Jack Nicholson?''

''Yeah, right,'' said Jack and then he looked at Lou. ''I don't know why I'm going to do this, but here goes. You fellas do know that if Magic played for the Celtics, they would have won that game tonight by fifty points, and that hunk of plywood they play in would be filled with better people than you boys.''

Cliff stood up, pulled up his pants, and Jack realized he was in for a mouthful. ''Sir, may I remind you that's the Gah-den you're talking about there. You know the one with all the championship banners hanging from the ceiling. As for Magic and Larry, I really think there's no comparison. In Lar-Bird, you're talking about your basic complete player. He can go to his left; he can go to his right; he can pull up and hit the jumper; he can play the great D. He can do it all.''

But Jack had to have the last word. ''Those banners you talk about—what the rest of the world call the laundry of success. How many have the Celtics won since the Bird came to town? We're talking about winners, here, and Magic has been one ever since he beat Larry for the NCAA championship in 1979.''

''Yeah, well, how about the time . . .''

And on and on it goes, this persistent squabble about who is the better basketball player—Larry Bird or Magic Johnson. It is more than just good bar-room banter or mere dinner conversation, but it is by definition a debate with no apparent end or answer. From the bars of Beantown to the boutiques of Beverly Hills, someone, everyone, thinks he or she has the last word on the subject of Magic and the Bird. All this arguing has to mean just one thing: "Me and Larry's just different from everybody else," said Magic. Added Larry, "We realize we're the same type of player."

The great thing about arguments and sports is that no one ever has the last word. But the legendary basketball guru Pete Newell may have said it best. (He always does.) "These are two of the greatest players we've ever had, and even though Magic's a guard and Bird's a forward, they sure as heck realize comparisons are going to be made. Naturally, they want to be at their best. If you were Raquel Welch and you lived across the street from Marilyn Monroe, you'd make damn sure you looked good every time you went out the front door."

When you're talking Magic and Bird, you certainly aren't jawing about someone who is just another pretty face. In fact, what you have here are two of the glamour guys of the game. You can rap all you want about the tremendous numbers they have put up over the years and all those accomplishments that have earned them the majority of the league's "Most Valuable" awards since 1980. But if Magic and Bird, Bird and Magic, have been the Laurel and Hardy, the Ruth and Gehrig, the Redford and Newman, the Lone Ranger and Tonto of their craft, then they certainly are the Welch and Monroe as well. Pretty boys at their best. As the journal that chronicles such things in the athletic world—*Sports Illustrated*—has proven, Magic has been on the cover 13 times and Larry 12, and only swimsuit model Elle MacPherson is as popular. To watch Magic come down the court on the fast break, look one way, and pass around the back the other, is as much a thing of beauty as Larry clearing out one side of the lane, backing his defender toward the basket, and turning around to swish that semi-fadeaway jump shot.

Such have been the signs of the times in the National Basketball Association since Larry and Magic have come into the league. That was the 1979–1980 season when Magic was still predominantly known as Earvin and Larry was just another good player. In that season, Bird was named Rookie of the Year and Earvin was the Most Valuable Player in the NBA championship series when he led the Los Angeles Lakers to a world championship. Magic has played in 7 such series in the 9 years he has been a Laker and has won 5 titles. Larry has been in 5 championship series and led the Celtics to 3 titles. Magic has been named the playoff MVP 3 times; Larry twice. Bird has also been named the league's outstanding player by the rest of the players themselves 3 times; Magic once. The list goes on and so does the beat.

If you're a basketball fan or even just a sports fan, you've been party to this great debate in some way, shape, or form. There's plenty of debate to fuel the fire; even the two great ones have considered the idea themselves.

"What makes it really interesting," Magic said, "is that it's not like we're just two great scorers, because you can shut scorers down. We do so many other things. Even if one of us isn't scoring, we make our presence felt." Bird added, "When you think of the impact we have on a game, we both do the same things."

And although you've tried, there is no way to get the absolute, definitive last word about Magic and Bird. Their rivalry probably will be well-documented up until the time they are old men and battling it out in a

marathon game of Monopoly. They are as different as
they are similar, and whether you're a basketball fan, a
sports fan, or just a fan of greatness in general, you just
have to raise your glass and say *Cheers* to Magic and
the Bird.

You never know when you're going to get into one of
those arguments about who is better, so remember, no
one is truly an expert when it comes to this subject. In
the end, it's probably best to order one more round and
toast the fact that you have been privileged enough to
have been a part of the Bird-Magic era, the "Era of the
Eighties," if you will. To be sure, their lives have
crossed paths in more than a few coincidental moments.
Their's is one story with many chapters, but never a
dull moment.

Reams and reams of copy have been devoted to the
subject of Magic and the Bird; pages and pages of
magazines have compared and contrasted their greatness. They are every bit as well known in Paris, France,
as they are in Paris, Kentucky; in the universal language
that basketball has become, Bird and Magic are synony-
mous with success. So to argue the point about who is
better is really not doing justice to either of these great
talents. Suffice to say they are together as one—ebony
and ivory—the most wonderful thing that has ever happened to this most wonderful sport. Consider the fact
that because of Magic it doesn't matter if you're 6' 9"—
you can still play that one position that has complete
control of the game. Point guard is no longer reserved
for short people. And then because of Bird, there will
always be hope for slow white guys who don't jump
very well to be able to play the game.

As Bob Ryan, the scholarly basketball writer for the

Boston Globe, pointed out about Magic and Bird, "They can only be compared to each other." Such is a good enough reason to put them in a class by themselves, but if you really want to be able to belly up to the bar some day and act like you know what you're talking about, start paying attention to the little things these guys do that have such a big impact. Bird, for example, can pull down a rebound, spin, and throw a perfect lead pass to Danny Ainge streaking downcourt for a lay-up—left-handed. Magic can pull down a rebound, dribble in and out of traffic, close in on the basket, then swish a hook shot—left-handed. It's almost scary, all the things that Magic and Larry can do that no one else can. They can only be compared to each other.

Perhaps the greatest testimony to their success is that they don't look great when they do such great things. Magic doesn't appear to be lightning-quick when he's leading the fast break in the way you'd think of Michael Jordan or Isiah Thomas as quick. Speed thrills, of course, but not so much as the Magic Man pulling up at the foul line and throwing the ball behind his back or through his legs to James Worthy or Jamaal Wilkes for a breakaway slam dunk. And the way Bird can take a pass on the wing and suddenly feed Robert Parish or Kevin McHale for an easy lay-up makes it seem as though the ball doesn't even touch his hands. Some players love to get out on the break and see only Bird between themselves and the basket. But Larry toys with the opposition by letting a player go by, then blocking the ball from behind without even jumping. The truly gifted ones make up the moves as the play progresses, so chances are you have rarely seen Larry or Magic do the same thing twice.

It's possible to ramble on forever about the memorable things these guys have done. But then, there's so much more to them than just endless raving. As Elgin Baylor, a former Laker who is now the general manager of the Los Angeles Clippers, said, "If you're talking about the greatest all-around player in the game, you're talking Bird or Magic." As the word of mouth from Johnson himself goes, "We respect each other's talent. It's a comfortable feeling, like you don't mind being in the same room with him. In the beginning, it wasn't always that way—there definitely was a rivalry. That's always going to be there. But it's no personal battle, me against him. He's the best, so you've got bring your best. The boy is bad."

The tale of Bird and Magic includes the good, the bad, and the ugly. For each, life was simple as a youngster. Before they emerged as high school sensations, Magic and Bird played ball for the fun of it. Magic used to shovel the snow off the court in the middle of winter so he could go outside and shoot. The routine wasn't complex: school, come home, get your homework done, then go play ball. For Bird it wasn't much different. There were days when he would pick up a bucket of Kentucky Fried Chicken, take it to the court, and shoot until it was time to go home for dinner. That's how he got to be so finger-licking good. When the ballplaying was finished, the little things made these guys happy; there were no problems with other temptations. Magic would stand on the corner of Middle and Williams streets in Lansing, Michigan with 3 of his friends, dancing and singing to "My Girl." Larry always liked to go off with his friends fishing. He still does.

They will always been devoted to their hometowns. Bird will forever be the Hick from French Lick, Indiana, where he still makes his home in the off-season. So it's no wonder that each wound up at a college right down the road from home: Magic at Michigan State in East Lansing and Larry at Indiana State in Terre Haute. Accordingly, perhaps, it wasn't so much of a coincidence that Michigan State played Indiana State for the National Collegiate Championship in 1979, the year before each athlete turned professional.

With the good came the bad and the ugly (what little of it there was). Magic had an untimely relationship that eventually produced a child out of wedlock. Larry rushed into a marriage his freshman year in college and wound up with a divorce and a daughter he has rarely been allowed to see. Bird also suffered with an alcoholic father who eventually committed suicide.

But if there's one thing you must understand about Magic and the Bird, it's that each is especially devoted to his home and his family. You're talking about a couple of mama's boys here. Christine Johnson not only cooks meals for her son when she visits him—she cooks for the whole team. When the Lakers played in Detroit for the 1988 NBA Championship, Christine made dinner for the Lakers and brought it to them in their locker room.

Larry is so much like his mother Georgia that most people say that's where his competitive obstinance comes from. He has become such a symbol of success for both French Lick and Terre Haute that "Larry Bird Boulevard" runs right through the center of each town.

If they went to college as hometown heroes, Magic and Bird both left college as national heroes. Perhaps no one knew that the evening of March 27, 1979 would be the night that the 2 great ones would write the first chapter of their legendary story. But what they did in college established for each an on-the-court personality that has drawn them together ever since. The only game Larry's Indiana State team lost his senior year was to Magic's team. And it was only appropriate that Magic would leave college 2 years early so he could come into the league the same time as Larry. Or perhaps it was destiny.

Of course, only in the National Basketball Association would we find out just how good Larry and Magic could be. Auerbach thought Bird was so good that he used his first pick in the annual college draft the year *before* Bird graduated to pick him. Perhaps that was best, for it saved some poor soul from having to decide who to pick first in the 1979 draft. So Magic, who was so unproven that they called him Earvin back then, went to the Lakers, who had no other choice. Not coincidentally, the NBA title also went to the Lakers the following season. But as Bird was awarded the honor for being the league's top rookie and Magic was named the Most Valuable Player of the playoffs, these were only signs of the times.

As mere babes in the woods—or the trees, as the NBA's big guys are called—both Earvin and Larry had considerable maturing to undergo. Call the years from 1981 through 1983, then, their growth period or wonder years. During that time, Magic helped the Lakers to another title and Larry did likewise for the Celtics. But they were only second-tier superstars at that point, one notch below Julius Erving, Moses Malone, and Kareem Abdul-Jabbar, the trio who'd each won a Most Valuable Player award during those wonder years.

Another thing you have to realize about Magic and the Bird is that they each have that rare ability to see the game one step ahead of everyone else. With that thought in mind, then, could it be possible that they were just toying with basketball fans their first 3 years in the league? During that time, one thing or another kept the ultimate from taking place: Magic and Larry squaring off for the NBA title. Entire teams play the game, but early on even the most unsuspecting fanatic couldn't help but fantasizing about Larry and Magic playing one-on-one for it all.

In June of 1984 it finally happened. The Lakers met the Celtics for the championship. "Me and Larry at last," Magic was heard to say. It took until the final game of the best-of-7 series before the Celtics actually took the championship right out from under the Lakers. As Magic looked back on it, he gave Boston the title, and this phase of his life changed his entire career.

It was also a time when Larry was on the verge of making his career perhaps the greatest of all time. George Orwell knew the year 1984 was special, for it was the year in which Bird won the first of 3 straight Most Valuable Players awards. Suddenly, kids on playgrounds from Boston to Beverly Hills were reaching down and rubbing their hands on their shoes to imitate the Bird. Suddenly, it was fashionable again to be a good outside shooter and not just someone who could run and dunk. Suddenly, it was fashionable again to be white and a superb basketball player.

Of all the great moments, however—and as you will see there are many—Magic and Bird made their mark on professional basketball with a 2-year performance on center stage. They were the stars of the show when Bird and Boston conned Los Angeles out of the title in 1984, and they were in the limelight and spotlight as the Lakers stole the final bow in what was supposed to be Boston's encore in 1985. NBA action was never more fantastic than when the Lakers and the Celtics played those 2 magnificent back-to-back 7-game series for the championship. Even if Magic and Bird weren't yet the 2 greatest players in the game, they had already been part and party to the 2 greatest championship seasons in the game.

By the 1986 season, they were a certified phenomenon. Earvin was now "Magic," with a effervescent smile that made watching the game as much fun as playing it. He had spawned a new style of how to play, or at least made it part of the popular culture. Fast-break basketball—the way Magic ran the Lakers—was nothing more than the way he and the boys back in Lansing used to go at it on the playgrounds. Flash was fun, and making the pass to lead to the open lay-up was just as important as looking good and looking cool doing so. It was a style so utterly deceptive and effective—being heroic rather than a hot dog. Others, like Isiah Thomas of the Detroit Pistons, have helped Magic make this the predominant style of play. But here was Johnson doing all these sensational things, and he was 6'9". Earvin Johnson gave new meaning to what it was to be a guard.

There aren't many players who can define or redefine a position and a style of play. Bird has done so just like Magic. He loved to shoot—and he worked very hard at it all his life—so that shooting became a thing of beauty when Larry did it; he provided the pinnacle. There were good shooters before, but now there was Bird. He was the kind of guy who loved it so much he went out before every game and practiced for hours. He always did that. In one 48-hour span he once took 323 shots. He made 274 of them. But what's amazing was that he did so many other things so well. He could pass—not as flashy as Magic—but incredibly efficiently. He rebounded, he played defense, he blocked shots, he made steals. Auerbach never thought a single forward could dominate pro ball so overwhelmingly, but, then, Bird gave new meaning to what it was to be a forward.

No question, Bird and Magic had become the leaders of the pack. Magic started his annual summer all-star game to benefit the United Negro College Fund, and all the best players came to L.A. to be a part of it. Ever the generous one, Earvin also organized such efforts as rallying the rest of the all-stars to donate their game bonuses to help feed people in Ethiopia. He became perhaps the most well-liked player in the league, and his travels with good friends Isiah Thomas and Mark Aguirre of the Dallas Mavericks certainly became part of the lore that has come to be associated with Johnson.

This is one department in which Larry didn't try to compete. Never needed to. Back home in French Lick all the old boys always have said that Larry's the best friend they've ever had. (That's one of the things he takes great pride in.) But while the rest of the players never hesitated to talk about their love for Magic, what they had for Bird seemed to be of another emotion. Silent infatuation may have been what it was, for they simply voted him the best player in the league each year and left it at that.

In 1986, Bird was the greatest, and so were the Celtics as he took them to their third title since his arrival in Boston. The reign didn't last long, however, as Magic came up with his MVP season in 1987 as the Lakers ran away with the championship. The next year he willed them to the title again and in the process helped achieve a place for the Lakers as one of the greatest teams in the history of the game.

But even 9 years into their careers, it was a pretty good bet that history was still in the making. In fact, by 1988 both Bird and Magic were only beginning to exhibit the longevity of their prowess. Even though the Celtics didn't play the Lakers for the championship that season, it was Bird's best year statistically since he first won the MVP award. As for Magic, he kept on trucking down the middle of the court, looking in Worthy's direction before dishing off to Byron Scott for the lay-up.

Likewise, it's a pretty good bet that this great debate over who is the greatest player in the game will continue. The good doctor of basketball himself, Julius Erving, said once that Bird was the greatest player he ever played against or with. Moments later he could be heard saying the same thing about the Magic Man. Frankly, it will become apparent that there never will be enough words to fully explain the aura of the Magic-Bird era. Henceforth, hopefully, may come the answers to everything you've wanted to know about Larry and Magic but never had the opportunity to ask. So if the opportunity to make a wager on the overwhelming question of who is better presents itself promptly, don't bet on it yet. Make it worth your while.

2.

Morning Glory

THE SUN CAME UP ON THIS SLEEPY LITTLE TOWN, WHICH may have been a sign from God. It was daybreak, and it meant the little boy could rise up and proceed to live out his dreams. The same thing that had made all his nights so sleepless again kept him awake the night before as well; the same old thought that was too real to be a dream. In bed, he could only think about basketball, for life was always darkest before dawn. The midnight runs up and down the court were mere mind games, something to make him even more restless. So he greeted the dawning of each new day like the dawning of a new era, because when the sun was shining, life was happy and oh so simple.

As little boys, Larry Bird and Magic Johnson were each afflicted with this would-be morning sickness. As soon as morning had broken, they made a break for the courts. All they wanted to do was play, so much so that to them basketball was the stuff dreams were made of. But, then, wasn't this one of those dreams that comes right from the heart of the heartland? East Lansing, Michigan, and French Lick, Indiana, are so much a part of the heartland of this country that the idea of both Magic and Larry waking up at dawn to play ball each morning is the stuff of which America's dreams are made.

There were many mornings back in Lansing when Christine or Earvin Sr. would walk into their son's room to get him up for school. But the bed was more often than not empty; Earvin Jr., whose nickname was "June Bug" back then, was already at the schoolyard courts, taking his best shot at making his dream come true. "People thought I was crazy. They really seriously did," said Magic. "It would be seven-thirty in the morning and they'd be going to work, and they'd say, 'There's that crazy June Bug, hoopin.' "

And wouldn't it figure that Larry acted the same way as a kid. By the time he was well into his pro career, Bird's exploits as a sleeper were legendary. But it hadn't always been that way. He didn't have to look for playmates, considering that he grew up with 5 brothers who could have formed their own all-star team. "I'd get up in the morning, and the first thing on my mind would be playing ball," Larry has said more than a few times.

And so play ball they did, which is why Larry and Magic have always seemed so youthful when they're out there on the court. Sometimes it seems like the way they grew up was a dream. But even for them, life was not without its rude awakenings. The important thing to remember, however, was that no matter what adversities they had to overcome, both Magic and the Bird had just enough heart to never lose sight of the dream.

Larry Joe Bird was born a blond bombshell (no mustache yet) in more ways then one. On December 7, 1956, 15 years after the bombing at Pearl Harbor, Georgia and Joe Bird brought the fourth of their 6 children into the world. The most ceremonious occasion in Larry's young life came at Christmas when he was 4 years old. Years later it would be known as his greatest gift; as Bird remembered, that was the time he was given his first basketball.

"My ball was one of those cheap rubber balls. I was so proud of it that I stayed up for hours bouncing it. I left it by the stove that night, and when I got up it had a great big knot on it. My parents got me another ball, and I remember that I wore that one completely out."

As those who have ever played against Larry or merely watched him play must know, you can't stop Larry Bird just by taking the ball out of his hands. No one moves better without the ball, and the development of such a talent tantamount to being among the greatest in the game might as well be attributed to his 2 older brothers, Mark and Mike. When you play with your older brothers you have to realize they're not going to pass to you very much, and it's not difficult to imagine what Larry went through in those family affairs in order to get his hands on the ball.

Nor were baskets easy to come by, which merely prompted the Bird men to be creative. Before this flock had a basketball hoop to play with, they used a coffee can. "We tried to shoot one of those small sponge-rubber balls through it," Larry recounted. "But basketball wasn't my only love. We played lots of baseball, softball, rubber ball—we played ball all the time."

Consequently, Bird's introduction to organized basketball was nothing out of the ordinary. Even today, many little boys—and a lot of girls—in Indiana grow up playing basketball. Hollywood leads us to believe that Indiana is nothing more than one small town after another in which life revolves around, if not above, the rim. If that is the case then Bird is an original Hoosier, and in French Lick he is bigger then the game itself. In his hometown, there was a program called "Biddy Ball," a standard Saturday service in which the players from the high school team taught fourth, fifth, and sixth graders the basics of the game.

"You know, the proper way to shoot, the basic passes, how to box out on rebounds," Larry explained. "Just the fundamental things." It was a fundamental program. It still is. Biddy Ball is alive and well in French Lick, where nowadays many little boys—and a lot of girls—bend down to rub their hands on their shoes and practice hard in an attempt to become the next Larry Bird.

From Biddy Ball, the road led to high school ball, where Larry was merely following in the footsteps of his brothers. Mike, the oldest, was 6'2", and nothing more than a role player on the Springs Valley High varsity team. But Mark, who is 3 years older than Larry, was a big man, a guy who could really play the game. Mark's idol was Bill Walton, who at the time was the center for UCLA, the dominant college team in the country. As boys will be boys, there were many a time when Larry and Mark would live out the dream of UCLA taking on the rest of the country. Perhaps it was no coincidence that Larry represented every other team in the country in this glorified game. Walton would eventually be Larry's teammate in Boston—which makes you believe that dreams actually do come true. But at this point Larry's idol was Mark. Mark wore number 33 first. He was the inspiration for Larry to improve his game, and it is more than fair to say that Mark's presence induced Larry to become a true player and competitor.

When Mark graduated from Springs Valley, Larry seemed sure to be the next Bird who would soar. By the time he was a sophomore, Larry was 6'1" and had already developed some of the silky-smooth moves that he flaunted so effortlessly in the years to come. At age 15, most good athletes are lucky to be coordinated enough to jump off their left foot when going up for a lay-up. Larry was already shooting with his left hand. More importantly, this was an integral point in the development of Bird's game. As a guard, he had to learn to pass the ball, which is amusing only because the way Larry grew to become so proficient at it would seem to indicate that this quality was inbred. Indeed, he was already showing he was a thoroughbred when it came to hoops, and the only thing that slowed him down was a broken left ankle early in the season.

Even then it was impossible to shut the Bird Man down completely, for even in a cast he would come to the gym and work on his shooting. (Perhaps that explained how he became such a good off-balance shooter.) By season's end, Larry wasn't completely healed, but some part of Bird in the lineup was better than no Bird. This was the Indiana High School Basketball Tournament, and any true Hoosier could overcome an injury to be part of the extravaganza. In the first round of the tournament, known as the sectional, Springs Valley was trailing with a minute left when Larry was fouled. He hit the 2 free throws to win the game. "I remember that Mark hit all four of his free throws in the state tournament," said Larry, speaking of his incentive. "So I had to hit mine."

The Larry Bird legend was growing, and so was Larry Bird. As a junior at Springs Valley, he grew to 6'3", and he played center, forward, and guard that year. The season ended with a loss in the sectional round of the state tournament, but basketball did not end for Bird there. During the summer he would be up with the sun, practicing and shooting, and it must have been a good practice—by the time Larry was a senior he stood 6'7". Springs Valley had a new coach named Gary Holland, who worked Bird at forward and center and helped him add deceptive post moves to his game. The quick drop-step he has fashioned first became a usable commodity that year when Larry averaged 30.6 points, 20 rebounds, and 5 assists per game. In a single 32-minute game that season he once pulled down 38 rebounds; scoring 50 points in a single contest happened more than a few times.

Such exploits, however, were never very important to Joe and Georgia Bird's family. When you have 6 children—after Mike and Mark is the only girl, Linda, then comes Larry and younger brothers Jeff and Eddie—chances are that making ends meet is a much higher priority. And the way things were with the Birds, providing for the family came before basketball. The first time Larry went to see Mark play in high school was his last game. "My father was proud of us, but he didn't go see us play," Larry reasoned. "Dad didn't like crowds either."

Perhaps that is where Larry's drive and determination to succeed came from. Sometimes the Bird family was so poor that Larry had to go live with his grandmother, Lizzie Kerns. Family was first and foremost for Bird, and he loved his grandmother so much it didn't make a difference that she didn't even have a telephone.

Guys like Larry Bird never forget where they come from, and because of his beginnings this man has worked hard to make himself what he is. He is not so different from any other poor kid; in many ways they all have a dream to someday make a million dollars. And if it weren't basketball, then Larry would have found some other way to make his dream come true. "It motivates me to this day," Bird once said of the poverty he endured in his childhood.

There were nights when even though the Birds had enough coal to stay warm, the old furnace would break down and fill the house with black smoke. Joe Bird would get up and try and fix things, but perhaps he was too often trying to fix things. It's not that he didn't love his family—as Larry has mentioned, he knew his father was always proud of him. One day, Joe even promised Larry 20 dollars if he made the freshmen basketball team at Springs Valley. Then again, he never spent much time just shooting around with his boys.

Joe was preoccupied with other obsessions, the most dangerous of which was alcohol. This was a man who was very well known for his ability with his hands (perhaps that is where Larry acquired his soft touch). Joe worked as a wood finisher for the Kimball Piano and Organ Company, which was the major source of industry in the greater French Lick-Orange County metropolitan area. He may not have seemed like much of a role model, but Joe Bird was nevertheless a significant role player in Larry's life. Some of those who knew Joe and Larry say many of the son's strong principles came from his father. And it's not as if Joe didn't make an impression on his boy.

"I remember one time when I was thirteen or fourteen and my father came home with an ankle all black and blue and out to here," recounted Bird to *Sports Illustrated* senior writer Frank Deford. "[It was so swollen] he needed me and my brother just to get his boot off, and he was in awful pain. But the next morning he got the boot back on and went to work. That really made an impression on me."

If his life is looked at as a dream, then it would only figure that Larry combined the best, most vibrant, and emotional aspects of each of his parents to form his personality. And if Larry is driven and compelled, his mother Georgia is downright relentless. If Larry is mad at someone for 2 days, Georgia will be mad for 2 months. But as Larry Bird never failed those who needed him most when it came to the crunch, Georgia Bird was always there for her family, especially at munch time.

"I remember she worked a hundred hours a week and made a hundred dollars, and then had to go to the store and had to buy a hundred and twenty dollars-worth of food," Bird said. "If there was a payment due to the bank, and we needed shoes, she'd get the shoes and then deal with the bank. I don't mean she wouldn't pay the bank, but the children always came first."

That's the way things are in French Lick, where the most important thing is keeping your feet firmly planted on the ground. And if for no other reason, that is why Larry will always be the favorite son of French Lick.

And that is also why he still spends every minute of the off-season in French Lick. Bird was actually born in French Lick's sister-city of West Baden, but its populace always has been small enough to be engulfed by French Lick, which is hardly one of Orange County, Indiana's typical communities.

The town has approximately 2,265 people, all of whom have definite ideas about what the good life is. In some quaint, unobtrusive way, French Lick is in the center of an urban triangle. Evansville, Indiana, and Louisville, Kentucky, to the south and Bloomington to the north leave French Lick in its own little world. No interstates pass near the town, which was nationally renowned long before Larry Bird ever played basketball.

Springs Valley is known as that because of its mineral springs, and as a result French Lick and West Baden have widespread reputations as resort towns. Once it was even Vegas-like in its attractions, and rumor has it that everyone from Al Capone to some of the nation's presidents used to vacation there. The Springs Hotel is legendary and still draws a pretty crowd every summer, when people like to make use of the mineral springs. Besides the Springs Hotel and the Kimball Piano and Organ Company, the only other major source of business is Pluto Water, which was produced from the water running through the mineral springs. For almost 75 years, the largest enterprise in French Lick may very well have been the bottling and selling of the laxative made from the local water with an advertising pitch of "If nature won't, Pluto will."

But Georgia Bird never saw the inside of the Springs Hotel until Larry was invited there for a basketball banquet. Which is not to say that Larry didn't have use for the good life. You might be under the impression that Larry developed his game playing against all the other local Hoosiers, but that semi-fadeaway jumper made its first appearance in pickup games against the blacks who made up the staff at the Springs Hotel.

By the 1970s Pluto had switched to manufacturing household cleaning products, and the Springs Hotel lost most of its luster. The glory was gone from the valley, which prompted many of the young people to move out. But not Larry Bird. "I've always enjoyed French Lick, and I could care less what they say about it." So Larry will always go drinking with the boys on Thursday nights, and he doesn't feel it's necessary to always pick up the tab. Perhaps the best part of the dream is that he will wind up permanently in French Lick, where the important things are going fishing, painting grandma's house, or just cruising around with his good friend, Tony Clark.

Clark is now a radio executive in Terre Haute, and he knows what made Bird the way he is. Clark said in *Sports Illustrated*, "Larry epitomizes the word friend. You really don't have to know anything else about him."

Perhaps only among the hometown folks is it possible to separate the dreams from reality. In fact, Lansing, Michigan, is one of the few places where Magic can be Earvin, and those who knew him when would argue that "Magic" refers more to the kind of effect he had on people than what he did with a basketball in his hands.

Charles Tucker is a clinical psychologist who met Earvin when he was working in the Lansing school system. A long-time friend like Tucker, whom Earvin calls his personal mentor, remembers the best side of Johnson when he first met Earvin an energetic eighth grader. "He was the kind of kid adults went out of their way to help, because it was obvious he wanted to make something of himself. He was always smiling, always saying, 'Let's go.' I don't like all that high-pollution attitude. That's not the kind of person Earvin is."

Johnson developed more than his winning ways in Lansing—he developed his winning attitude there. "If you were supposed to play basketball with him," Tucker remembered, "he'd always be there early." By the time he was playing for the Everett High School varsity team, Johnson was the best all-around player. He could shoot, he could rebound, he could handle the ball; as someone once said, he could do it all. It was not uncommon for him to bring the ball upcourt for Everett, then go underneath the basket and play center. It was then that a local sportswriter first called him "Magic," and the effect he had on his teammates was that they would stand around and watch him do it all. "You know it used to kill me when Earvin came into the pros and they said he couldn't shoot," said Earvin Sr. "When he was in high school, that's practically all the boy did."

Eventually Earvin learned to pass, because as Tucker said, "[He] realized if he did all the scoring, it alienated the opposing players. So he started passing the ball, and big as he was, he could pass the ball easily. And he really enjoyed it. He also found it was easier to win that way."

Perhaps Magic became so good at doing it all because that's the way he learned the game. On the Main

Street Elementary School playground in Lansing, Earvin would pass the time by acting out his dream. In the imaginary game, Magic had to do it all because he played for both of the teams. This was his version of the championship of the entire civilized world of hoops, and it would always be his favorite team, the Philadelphia 76ers, against his brother's favorite team, the New York Knicks.

"I loved Philadelphia, see, and I always made sure they won the game. I'd make sure I missed a last-second shot and then Wilt Chamberlain would come down and dunk it. Except, I'd lay it up."

If Earvin was born to play ball, then it was not long after June 14, 1959—when he emerged at the fighting weight of 7½ pounds—that he took to the playground. With his eldest brother Larry, who is 2 years older, and his other brother Quincy, who is one year older, Earvin would ramble up and down the court. Imagine Larry on one wing and Quincy on the other as if they were playing the part of his future Laker teammates on the fast break. Except Earvin didn't pass too much. If they needed a fourth on Sundays, Earvin Sr. would join them.

"He's been fooling around with a basketball ever since I can remember, when he was a little fella," said the elder Earvin. "He played other sports, too, some football, a little baseball, but he always liked basketball best. They were at the Main Street Elementary School every morning, even on Sunday. I played with them sometimes, because I was a pretty fair player in my day."

Actually, it was Earvin Sr. who taught his boy the finer points of the game. When Magic wasn't playing, he would sit by his father and watch hoops on television. Never was there a better time for Earvin to have a Coke and a smile, for he still looks back on those moments as the fondest memories of his childhood. Father and son have never been short on time to talk and have a few laughs, even if in those early days it was more often serious.

"My father would point out things to me, like Oscar [Robertson] taking a smaller guard underneath, or the pick and roll," Magic remembered. "By the time I started playing organized ball, if the coach asked whether anybody knew how to do a three-man weave or a left-handed lay-up, I was the first one up. He taught me quite a bit."

But what developed more than Magic's propensity to play the game during those times was a friendship. Because of a fear of flying, Earvin Sr., a factory worker for 30 years at Fisher Auto Body in Lansing (who, like Joe Bird, was good with his hands), never went to see Magic play much outside of Lansing. By the time Earvin Jr. had become so good at the game, though, basketball became secondary in their relationship. Picture the two Earvins sauntering down Middle Street talking about everything under the sun. This is a father-son relationship that most other people merely dream about.

"My dad, you see, he's more than my dad. He's my partner. We hang out. It's more like two buddies than a father-son thing with us. We go out together. We talk for hours. He knows that I don't always feel like talking, and sometimes we just walk. He knows me better than anybody."

Earvin Sr., and Christine brought 7 children into this world, so Christine developed her knack for cooking for big groups right in her own kitchen. Sweet potatoes is one of her specialties and will always be one of Magic's favorites. Behind Larry, Quincy, and Magic came Pearl one year later; Kim 2 years after that; and one year later the twins Evelyn and Yvonne. There was a time when Evelyn was so good for the Everett team that she was the female "Magic." So the dinner table was more of a training table; not the place you'd want to be if it was Thanksgiving and you were hungry, though the Johnsons are the type of people who pride themselves on always having room for one more. Earvin Sr. is a Brook Haven, Mississippi, native, and both he and Christine bred that good-natured hospitality that is so much a part of Earvin Jr. in all their children. In fact, it isn't hard to imagine sitting around the table with the family and seeing 9 Johnsons smiling brightly at you.

But for many reasons—besides a smile that just wouldn't quit—Magic was special. Like the Larry Bird lore, there are plenty of stories about Magic that are all true. He did indeed shovel the snow off the playground courts in the middle of winter, and in the summertime he played until dark. Magic never needed an opponent. It was as if even back then he was telling the coach, "Just give me the ball, and I'll make something happen."

He could always make people smile, too, especially the dozens who used to gather around the Main Street Elementary School playground to watch him strut his stuff. The baskets on the playground were just 8 feet high, so Magic could jam even in his early years when jamming not only meant stuffing the ball through the hoop but turning up the radio, taking the rock, and letting it roll. The sound of the bouncing ball was music to the Magic Man's ears, as he and whichever four buddies he happened to team up with on any given day would hold the court for hours.

In the genre of pickup basketball, 5-on-5 games play on until one team reaches 15 or 16 baskets. That team becomes the winner, and the other team is left calling "winners," which means being relegated to the next game or the game after or—as was the case at Main Street—the game after that. If you came out to the playground, you wanted to be on Magic's team because you never had to call "winners." And ever since those games, he continued to perfect the style that is all his own. "[The playground] was always packed with guys wanting to play," Earvin said, "so the only way you could hold the court was to win. That's why we went for the drives and the sure two instead of the outside shots."

It didn't take Earvin long to outgrow the competition on the playground, and in ninth grade he took the magic act to the Michigan State intramural building in East Lansing. "The first time I just came to watch, really." But Michigan State star Terry Furlow knew Earvin was something special when he picked him to play on his team. "I was scared, but Terry was braggin' on me, calling me his main man."

The legend of the "Magic Man" was only beginning to grow, and at that point in his life so was Earvin. By seventh grade, he was already 5'11", and in eighth grade he was a 6'3" tower of power. It isn't hard to spot Earvin in any of his grade school class pictures. He is the one in the center of the back row who is about a head taller than everyone else. In ninth grade, Earvin was 6'5" and definitely the head of the class. "We had to keep buying him new clothes because he grew out of them so fast," said Earvin Sr.

He was already a legend in Lansing. By the time he went to Everett, Earvin didn't have to go looking for games—the games came looking for him. He never again had to play alone. One of his frequent one-on-one partners was Jay Vincent, who played with Earvin at Michigan State and eventually went on to star for the Dallas Mavericks and the Denver Nuggets in the NBA. In high school, Earvin and Jay used to hang together and were easily recognized on playgrounds and in gymnasiums as 2 of "the baddest cats in town."

While Earvin was the main man at Everett, Vincent became the top dog at cross-town rival Eastern High. Once the 2 squared off in a game at Jenison Field House where Michigan State played all its home games. All 9,886 seats were filled, and it was the first time Jenison had sold out in years. It would not be the last. There was also another Eastern-Everett game which was broadcast on local television. The ratings were just less than what they had been for that year's Super Bowl.

In addition to everything else, Earvin was a media man. As a senior at Everett, he averaged 28.8 points per game and 16.8 rebounds. He was the first 3-time All-State selection in the history of Michigan, and in those 3 years he scored 2,012 points. The final season he led Everett to a 27–1 record and the state Class A championship, an accomplishment which was the first of 3 (making him the answer to a trivia question).

After the season Magic toured Germany with a high school all-star team, and when he returned home, thousands of Michigan State rooters and boosters greeted him with signs urging him to play for the hometown university. Of course, Magic was the hometown boy every bit as much as was Bird, and when he did finally make the announcement to commit to Michigan State, the event received more local television coverage than President Gerald Ford had when he'd made a recent visit to Lansing.

That, however, doesn't fully describe the prominence of Earvin's prowess. One summer during high school, he went to visit relatives in Rocky Mount, North Carolina, and one day he went looking for some action. He came up against a 20-year-old who was also the "baddest cat on the playground" and very much part of the local legend. In this ultimate game of one-on-one, Earvin went down by 6 hoops quickly, and at that point he didn't even need the 20 dollars which had been bet on the game as incentive. Magic won the game, 15–8. The legend had been rewritten, for the local boys had just seen the magic act up close and personal. "He was really upset," Earvin recalled. "He even tried to get his friends to lend him more money, so he could play me again. But they wouldn't do it."

You see, the thing about both Larry and Magic is that the stories that seem like mere fabrication are really true; the dreams are indeed reality. But back then during those wonder years life was anything but a dream. In fact, those times make Larry smile as wide as Magic. It's those times when life was as good as it gets. Perhaps, then, they could only dream that life could get any better.

3

That Championship Season

THIS WAS THE ULTIMATE GAME OF ONE-ON-ONE. IN BAR rooms and living rooms across America the quandary already had been discussed; only at this time no one realized there would never be a readily available solution. What was to transpire during this last week of March 1979 was a duel of epic reporting. Larry Bird and Earvin Johnson were about to meet for the first time face to face, and the event promised to make for a night to remember and a fight to the finish.

Out of one corner came the Magic Man, wearing the green and white trunks and all pumped up for the occasion. In the other corner was the Bird, clad in blue and white and ready to take his counterpart's best 1–2 punch. They shook hands and went at it.

Magic took the first shot, straight from the hip. "I love it, love it to death," he had said. "Oooh, this is fun. I'm a fan of Larry Bird's because he does so many things well. But I can't get caught looking.''

Larry overcame that flurry, then responded with all the vehemence of a back-in-your-face jumper. "[Earvin's] probably laughing at the opponents. But I got to do what I got to do. I can't be laughing out there. Earvin's different. I just hope he's not laughing at me.''

Leave it to Earvin to take the last shot. "Larry is a good guy. We had fun and joked around when we played together once on an all all-star team. We're just different. I'm outgoing. I love people. I love conversation.''

In round one Magic had the last laugh, but this had just been a meeting of minds when they squared off in front of a hungry horde of press people the day before they were to court each other for the national collegiate championship. Magic was slightly more adept at handling this full-court press, and even then it seemed as though he was always able to get one up quickly on Larry before Bird would come soaring back just when it seemed he was down for the count. In the first of many fights to remember, Magic played his game of one-on-one upmanship in the process of leading Michigan State to a 75–64 victory over Indiana State on March 26, 1979 for the NCAA championship. Johnson may have had the last laugh as he outscored Bird 24 to 19, which netted him the honor as the Most Valuable Player of the competition. In the end, though, he could only smile at his foe—the nation's unanimous choice as the Player of the Year.

For no longer was it time to keep talking about it. That championship season of 1978–79 ended with the summit that had been anticipated perhaps as soon as the previous season had concluded. These were 2 guys who brought the thrill of victory to 2 schools that had known little more than the agony of defeat before their enrollment. As soon as Bird made the short trek north to Terre Haute, Indiana and the Indiana State University campus, and as soon as Johnson traveled across town to East Lansing, Michigan, home of Michigan State University, they were destined to be All-American boys. By the time they each led their teams to conference and regional championships in that 1979 season, they had become the featured attraction in the game everyone had been waiting for. As Magic said, it was America's game. "To have your name in all the newspapers in the country, you got to love it. All the parents from California to Germany know about it."

Most of the basketball world was watching when the 2 splendid superstars were deciding where they would spend their college years. There were times when both Larry and Earvin must have felt like the entire college basketball world was coming through their respective living rooms as part of the recruiting process. In such an endeavor, a coach visits a player's home and brings with him a briefcase full of promises. It's not hard to imagine Larry sitting there just nodding his head, probably wishing he was fishing, or Magic just smiling widely while someone made him an offer he supposedly couldn't refuse. But remember you're talking about one guy who averaged 30 points and 20 rebounds a game in high school and another who put up 28.8 points and pulled down 16.8 rebounds, so the basketball world needed both Larry and Earvin more than they needed it. At this point they had the world by the basketballs.

Representatives from more than 200 schools came

calling on Larry, while Earvin Sr. didn't quite remember how many contacted his son. "It seemed like three hundred or more," he said. But Earvin Jr. wanted nothing to do with this numbers game. Michigan State was just across town; he had played at Jenison Field House in high school, and he was already a local hero. It didn't even matter that long-time coach Gus Ganakas had recently been replaced by a newcomer from Montana named Judd Heathcote or that the Spartans had won more games than they lost in just 2 of the previous 10 seasons.

"I think all along Earvin had his mind made up to go to Michigan State," his father continued. "When they brought in a new coach, he started thinking about some other places, like the University of Michigan. But he's not sorry he chose Michigan State."

Added his son: "One of the reasons I came to Michigan State was that I love to be the underdog and rise to the occasion."

For Bird, the matter was slightly more complicated. In Indiana, most little boys want to grow up to star for the state's best university. The trouble is, Indiana has more great basketball schools per capita than any other state in the country. Notre Dame, Purdue, and Indiana usually dominate the local recruiting wars, but there is always plenty of talent left over for Indiana State, Ball State, and Evansville. When Larry was a senior, Bobby Knight, the much-sensationalized coach of Indiana University in Bloomington—50 miles from French Lick—came to his living room and did nothing more than sit in a chair and talk to Larry about playing for him. Larry liked the idea of Bloomington being close to home, and he also liked the IU players who came to visit French

Lick. So in the fall of 1974, he left for Bloomington to get his share of the Knight life.

Here was Bird, not really a social butterfly, at a campus with far more people than he was accustomed to in his hometown. Suddenly, he was feeling small town and small time. He could see the difference between himself and the rest of the campus community as soon as he moved into his dormitory room. After 24 days, he packed what little clothes he'd brought and headed back to French Lick. He never did play for Knight. "I had a few pairs of pants, a few shirts, and not much else. [My roommate's] stuff took up ninety-five percent of the closet, and it's not like he was all that rich. Everywhere I looked, it was like that. I couldn't cope." Said Knight: "It was a damn mistake I made, letting him get away."

Leaving Bloomington only made matters worse for Bird. He returned home no longer a local hero, and he felt he'd let the locals down. His father committed suicide shortly after he came back, and that's when Larry pretty much hit rock bottom. As the Bird legend dictates, he went to work on a garbage truck in French Lick, but that was only part of his duties one day a week in his job with the sanitation department. Looking back, however, this could be where Bird gained an integral part of his overall persona. Back home, he learned about fortitude. He spent some of the days hurling garbage bags around with one of his best friends, Bezer Carnes, and realized how to make the best of a bad situation. "I loved that job," Bird said. "It was outdoors, you were around your friends. I felt like I was accomplishing something. How many times are you riding around your town wondering why they don't fix that or why they don't clean the streets up. I had the chance to do that. I had the chance to make my community better.''

Bird still had a mission to make the world a better place, though, and the best way to do that was through basketball. Georgia Bird and Lizzie Kerns wanted their boy to be happy, so they stopped all those coaches who came to see Larry that year right at the front door. But they also wanted their boy to give college another try.

Bob King had added the job of athletic director to his head coaching duties at Indiana State, and together with his dedicated assistant coach, Bill Hodges, he was intent on building a winning hoops program. They had some tradition on their side; not as much as Indiana or Notre Dame, but in 1946, 1947, and 1948, a virtual wizard of a coach named John Wooden, who went on to become the greatest in the college game in leading UCLA to 10 straight national championships, had run things in Terre Haute. Hodges had been particularly relentless in pursuing Bird before he went to Indiana, and he knew that Bird would be the foundation necessary to building a winning tradition. Georgia was the immediate obstacle to overcome, and one time she asked Hodges, "Why are you bothering him? He doesn't want to go to school. Leave him alone." Then she made sure to whisper to King before he left, "But I hope you can talk him into going."

King said the hardest part of recruiting Bird was not getting him to go to ISU, but getting him to go to school at all. In 1975, Bird decided to give another old college try and took off for Terre Haute, where he would have to sit out a year after transferring (as the NCAA rules specified).

College basketball was a whole new world for both Bird and Johnson. Men of their attributes have no problems dominating a high school basketball game, but at the next level it is rather difficult to come right in and do it all. Then again, that is how the truly great ones who play the game stand out from the rest. When you separate the men from the boys, you have what is known as an *impact player*; a boy who comes in and immediately proves himself to be a man, and one who makes his presence felt immediately.

Talk about impact. In Bird's first game for Indiana State, he scored 31 points, pulled down 15 rebounds, and dished out 8 assists in a victory over the Brazilian national team. As a freshman, Johnson averaged 20 points and 7 assists per game in leading Michigan State to its first Big Ten Conference championship since 1957. This was sudden impact.

The gospel according to Indiana State coach King: "He does everything well; we know he's the complete player." Then the coach added as a postscript, "We know he hasn't played a minute of college basketball yet."

The words out of Lansing were similar, for Johnson had made an immediate impression on everyone, including his teammates. Very few people ever forget the first time they met Earvin Johnson, Jr. "We needed something like this," said Spartan forward Greg Kelser, who was 2 years Johnson's senior yet considered him every bit his equal. "I don't think it took any adjustment because he was the new guy. He was so far advanced than any freshmen in the country. We understood this. We needed it."

The other measure of impact is how quickly you can

help turn the program around. In his first 2 games, Bird recorded the coveted triple double, in which a player posts numbers in double figures in the three major statistical categories; points, rebounds, and assists. Although the Basketball Hall of Fame does not include an exhibit on the history of the triple double, future research might well show that the concept was created in Bird's first game as a collegian. He had 31 points, 18 rebounds, and 10 assists in a 81–60 season-opening win over Chicago State, and then he added 22 points, 16 rebounds, and 10 assists in an 85–59 thrashing of St. Ambrose College the next game. Rarely had anyone ever come so close to the triple double so often before Bird. Unless it was Magic, who had 31 points, 8 rebounds, and 4 assists in an 87–83 win over Minnesota in the Big Ten opener.

This presented a feeling not really known in these 2 basketball corners of the country. ''After we beat Minnesota, I remember going back to my dorm room and telling my roommate, 'Man, I think we can do it. I think we can win the Big Ten.' '' The beat went on as Magic turned the Spartans from a 10–17 team the year before to a 25–5 club in the 1977–78 season.

Bird was in the process of working similar miracles at Indiana State. During an 8-game stretch of his initial season, Larry scored more than 40 points 8 times. He had 47 points to go with 18 rebounds in a 110–87 win over Missouri-St. Louis, and he duplicated that 47-point effort later in that season to lead the Sycamores to a 80–65 victory over Butler. Simple arithmetic tells you that in that game he scored more than half of his team's points, and further addition reveals that Larry had 59% of the team's points. Indiana State went from 13–12 the year before Bird played to 25–3 with him, and that was the best record in Terre Haute since 1947–48 when a man named John Wooden coached the Sycamores.

Michigan State, likewise, was experiencing new-found success with the Magic Man. He led the team to the finals of the Mideast Regional of the NCAA championship tournament in 1978 before the Spartans lost to eventual national champ Kentucky, 52–49. He was the only freshman named to any All-American team. He was a second-team All-American as named by the National Association of Basketball Coaches (NABC). His own coach, Heathcote, called him "the best player in all of basketball," and other coaches heaped similar praise upon Earvin, who averaged 17 points and more than 7 rebounds a game. "He was the finest freshman I've ever seen," said Fred Schaus in 1978, who was then the coach at Purdue. Added Johnny Orr, who was coaching at Michigan at the time, "It took the Spartans thirty years to get up there, and if he goes away, they're going right back down."

With Bird soaring, Indiana State was going up, up, and away. He most definitely was their superman, and his accomplishments his first year in college seemed almost superhuman. He was the third-leading scorer in the nation with a 32.8 average. Such a statistic made him just the twelfth player in NCAA history to average more than 30 points a game in a single sophomore season. He was named to All-American teams by both the Associated Press and United Press International, as well as the U.S. Basketball Coaches Association. Bird also added 13.3 rebounds per game, twelfth-best in the nation.

And he also brought immediate prominence to Indi-

ana State. The Hulman Civic Center, home of the Sycamores, was not exactly a hot spot on campus when the
basketball team was playing. But when the Bird came
to town, thousands and thousands more started piling
into the place.

Years later, of course, twice as many fans as can fit
into the Hulman Center claim they were there the night
Larry scored 45 points against Loyola of Chicago in the
middle of that 1976–77 season. By season's end, Indiana State garnered its first post-season tournament bid
ever. In the first round of the National Invitation Tournament (NIT), the Sycamores lost to Houston, 83–82,
in a game that will live in infamy more because of
Bird's 44 points than anything else.

It wasn't complete bliss for Bird, though. Just as his
life was coming back together, it fell apart again. In
1975, Bird rushed into a marriage he doesn't talk about
much. In 1977, the marriage collapsed, yet he discov-
ered that his ex-wife was pregnant. His daughter Corrie
was born just before the start of his junior year, but
since then he has rarely been allowed to have much
contact with her. Bird doesn't discuss this period, and
fortunately, a lovely young lady named Dinah Mattingly
came into Bird's life at about that time. Dinah has since
been Larry's loyal companion, so much so that she
probably is the all-time world leader in rebounding,
considering that she has spent so much time chasing
down Larry's misses from his persistent practice. ''There
have been a lot of nights when that girl did nothing but
pass that ball back to me,'' Bird said.

One thing about Bird, though, is that he is always
able to put everything behind him when he steps onto
the court. He proved that during the 1977–78 season,

when he led the Sycamores to a 23–9 record, another
NIT berth, and a banner campaign against the school's
toughest competition ever. He topped the 40-point mark
4 times, with a season-best 45 in a 93–77 win over
Central Michigan and another 45 in a 92–80 defeat of
Drake. He finished the season with a 30-point average
as the Sycamores beat Illinois State, 73–71, before
bowing out of the National Invitation Tournament with
a 57–56 loss to Rutgers. Bird was named a consensus
All-American by the A.P., UPI, the U.S. Basketball
Writers Association, and any group or publication with
enough clout to put out an All-American team. Bird is
probably the consumate consensus All-American. He
was second in the voting for the James Naismith trophy,
given to the top player in the nation by UPI, and he was
third in the balloting for the Adolph Rupp trophy, awarded
to A.P.'s Player of the Year. He was far and away the
best player in the Missouri Valley Conference that season and perhaps no more than a 12-ft jump shot from
being the best college player, ever.

Such a statistical breakdown is perhaps the best way—
maybe the only sufficient way—to document these college years leading up to that championship season.
Everything else that both Larry and Magic accomplished
was on such a spur of the moment, too quick for any
mortal media member to fully describe. For the most
part, observers were left speechless as Larry would
drive the lane and send a pass to an open teammate
behind his back or over his head. Magic elicited the
same response when he would pick the ball off the
defensive board, dribble the length of the court, and
send a pass to a streaking Spartan who often arrived at
the open spot the same time as the ball. But mere

numbers couldn't always do justice to what Magic or Bird accomplished as they set out on the path that merged with the 2 of them being the best players in the college game prior to that 1978–79 season.

"In Earvin's case you don't talk about the points he scores," Heathcote said, "but the points he produces. Not just the baskets and assists, but the first pass that makes the second pass possible."

With Bird, it wasn't always the points he scored that made the point. As Tulsa *Tribune* sportswriter Doug Darroch wrote, "Bird deflected a Tulsa pass . . . chased it to the sideline and dived to keep it in-bounds. He landed against the press table with one foot in somebody's soft drink. He did not get up immediately—he was shaken. But after walking around and rubbing his sore right arm, he was ready to dive into somebody else's soft drink."

This was most definitely the real thing. Bird and Johnson were getting ready to make the world of college basketball their own personal playground. For a brief moment it was fantasy land as the 2 of them actually teamed up together. In a college all-star game during the summer of 1978, the magical men spent about 2 minutes on the court together. As luck would have it, they were even out on the break together. In this 2-on-1, Magic dished to Bird who dished back to Magic for an easy lay-up. And if nothing else, this golden moment set the table for the season to come. Fans were beginning to salivate with thought of the upcoming year as most basketball prognosticators predicted it would be a feast for Michigan State and Indiana State and a famine for the rest of the nation.

The pre-season of college basketball—the time from

the end of November through holiday tournaments in December before conference play begins—only served to whet the collective appetites of America's fans. By the time the new year rolled in both the Spartans and Sycamores were rolling. Michigan State won the Far West Classic Tournament in Seattle and by january 2 fashioned a 7–1 record, making the club the nation's number one-ranked team in the wire service polls. Indiana State, ranked fifth, won its first 10 games and was 1 of 2 unbeaten teams in the land.

In the process, Bird was soaring and scoring, 29 points in addition to 19 rebounds in a 101–89 victory over Tulsa for that tenth win of the year. The Bird beat went on and was so closely monitored that even to this day you can still get a game-by-game description of all his points and rebounds any time you pick up an Indiana State basketball program.

All eyes were watching both Bird and Magic, which was enough incentive for Johnson to turn this season into show time. There was a warning sign when Earvin was about to move into gear; seeing his eyes light up meant trouble ahead for the opposition. When his eyes turned green it was time for the Spartans to get up and go on the fast break that made them so formidable. On January 4, 1979, the MSU opened their Big Ten Conference season in front of a sellout crowd at Jenison Field House. Wisconsin was still hanging tough late in the first half when Heathcote called over his point guard and requested him to turn on the magic. "The coach told me that we were going to spread the court and go to our passing game. But he added, 'If you want to dominate the game, go ahead and do it.' You know, if he gives me the green light like that, I've got to go for it.''

It wasn't long before he turned out the lights on Wisconsin. Magic scored 12 straight points late in the first half to turn a 2-point lead into a blowout. He finished with 21 points, 13 rebounds, and 14 assists, a collegiate best. Said Heathcote, "Earvin is probably the reason we won, but he is the reason we've won a lot of times.''

Every game of this final year in college made it a championship season. Whenever Bird or Johnson came to town, it provided enough hype and hoopla to turn it into a championship-like game for the opponent. Coaches would dig deep down into their play books to devise some type of strategy to hold Bird to 20 points or less. (That is, if a player is actually held to 20 points.) They were always treated with a full-court press as was the case when the Spartans came trucking into Champaign to take on third-ranked Illinois on January 11. It brought the best out of the local media, as David Condon of the Chicago *Tribune* wrote that morning, "Those who've played against him say Magic can be stopped only by miracles." And so it was that when Eddie Johnson hit a shot with time running out to give Illinois a 57–55 victory it was like the eighth wonder of the basketball world. Fans rushed on to the court at Champaign's Assembly Hall in a victory celebration that made it seem like their team had just won the national championship.

When other teams brought out their best, it seemed to bring out the best in Larry and Earvin. After the loss to Illinois, Michigan lost on another buzzer-beating jump shot at Purdue on January 13, but in the next game

Magic overcame foul trouble in the first half to score 20 of his game-high 22 points in the second half of a 82–58 must-win over Iowa.

In such situations Bird also showed his magic. Indiana State was trailing Creighton, 46–43, at the start of the second half of a crucial Missouri Valley Conference game when Bird let fly with a flurry of jumpers. He hit with his left, he hit with his right, he scored off the drive: 9 straight shots during the first 11 minutes of the second half. He finished with 29 points and the Sycamores survived with a 90–80 victory.

When things go well and your team is winning there is nothing better than being a fan, especially on campus. Students would rally around the dance floor at Bonnie and Clyde's disco in East Lansing to watch Magic do his other thing—his second-best moves have always come on the dance floor. And in Terre Haute, there was nothing better than seeing Larry walk by with his ever-present International Harvester baseball cap and blue jeans, just to have the chance to say, "Nice game."

Even when the cheers turned to tears, there were always Magic's and Bird's broad shoulders to cry on. Would Indiana State and Michigan State have been able to climb to the top of the mountain if at some point during this marvelous season the teams didn't encounter some setbacks? The Sycamores were still winning, and when they were the only unbeaten team in the nation by the last week of January, all of southern Indiana anticipated the team being ranked atop the wire-service polls. But on January 31, the rankings were released and Indiana State was still number 2. To Bird that only meant he had to try harder.

Such was also an opportunity to put the powers of

overcoming adversity to the test. Michigan State, for example, lost another heartbreaker, this time to Michigan on a free throw after regulation time had expired. Then on January 27, the Spartans lost at Northwestern, 83–65. Magic had a triple double with 26 points, 10 rebounds, and 10 assists, but Northwestern hadn't won a game in the Big Ten all season and the Wildcats would win only one more in 1979.

Perhaps, it was at the beginning of February when this championship season turned into just that. In a single leap or with a single bound, Larry and Earvin turned all fears back to cheers. What became most apparent in Magic's game was his ability to work the crowd, and so it didn't matter if he led the team in points, assists, or rebounds because he was always the head cheerleader. You talk about a quality that set both these guys apart from the rest of the college players—and this was it. Bird could drive the lane, carry 2 or 3 defenders to the hole, and softly scoop a left-handed bank shot off the glass and the Hulman Center would erupt. Magic would look one way, pass the other to net an easy lay-up, then run back down the court leading the cheers all the way.

In fact, on February 2, it may have been Earvin's ability to play to the crowd that made the difference. With 2:23 left in the first half of a game against Ohio State, Magic came down hard on his right ankle and suffered a sprain bad enough to force him to leave the game and the stadium. With the Spartans trailing in the second half, he emerged from the locker room and led them to victory. Operating on an apparent charge of adrenaline from a frenzied standing ovation, he scored 9 of his 23 points in the last 4 minutes to help force an overtime. Michigan State prevailed, 84–79, which in the end had Magic feeling no pain.

"At first the doctor and the trainer weren't going to let me come back," he said. "But when Ohio State took the lead I begged and begged them to let me play. This was the game right here. I said, 'We can't wait, we gotta go now.' I took a chance, but it worked."

Johnson's mere presence on the floor for a few minutes was enough to lift the Spartans to a 61–50 payback to Northwestern on February 3, and the next afternoon he was back in his usual rare form. With a national television audience looking on, Magic did it all, including 11 assists and some slick moves for the cameras in an 85–61 trashing of Kansas. "Even when Earvin is not one hundred percent, he does a lot of things for us," Heathcote said.

While Michigan State had climbed to 7–4 in the Big Ten and 14–5 overall, most of the country was waiting for Indiana State to take a fall. But some fan in Indiana felt that the Sycamores were blessed, and if Larry Bird weren't God in high-top sneakers then he was capable of reaping some divine intervention. Those folks were right, or so it seemed on the night of February 4, when the Sycamores' Bob Heaton threw in a desperation 50-foot shot to send a game at New Mexico State into overtime when State won 91–89. And then 2 nights later, Bird proved he was no mere mortal. Second-place Drake came to town and a victory would all but clinch the conference championship. The Bulldogs tried to hold Bird's jersey and they pushed him down. But they couldn't hold him down. Bird wound up with 33 points, 10 rebounds, and 10 assists for his third triple double of the season. Once more, 3 Drake players fouled out trying to hold him down. Perhaps he should have been thankful the Bulldogs didn't resort to biting.

When you're Earvin Johnson or Larry Bird you just have to do what it takes to win. As 13,365 fans screamed various things at him on February 8 in Iowa City, Magic hit 4 straight free throws before throwing a long pass to teammate Greg Kelser for the basket that sealed a 60–57 win over Iowa. For Magic this was the time of his college life. "I love it when it's winning time," he said. "I love it when the crowd is making all that noise and the ball goes through the net, and it's 'Ooooh.' "

On February 10, Indiana State beat Bradley 91–82 for its twenty-second straight victory, and Larry Bird didn't miss a shot. He took only 2 in the game; he needed to take only 2. Bradley put 3 defenders on him everywhere he went on this night except the bathroom. He did what he had to do, which meant grabbing 11 rebounds, most of them on the defensive end. After the short drought, Larry continued his reign by scoring 27 points, pulling down 19 rebounds and dishing out 5 assists in a 100–75 victory over West Texas State. This gave the Sycamores the Missouri Valley championship.

But to be more specific Larry Bird had led Indiana State and all its followers to a most promised land. Not that he made the promise, for where the public was concerned Bird took a vow of silence for this season. But every time Larry took the Hulman Center floor he looked at the Sycamores' massive student section and left the fans with a reassuring wink. For him this was tantamount to saying We're number one. On February 13, 1979, Indiana State was ranked number one in the nation by the Associated Press for the first time in school history. The phrase "first time in school history'' was pretty much a standard accompaniment to most of Bird's accomplishments during this season. But no matter what happened from this day forward, no one could take this day away from Indiana State. Sure, Magic had already been there; he has usually been the one to get there first. But now you had to have the feeling that Earvin was smiling in East Lansing because, being the great sportsman he was, he knew Larry's time was well past-due. Magic would settle the score once and for all later, but now Larry's victory was first and foremost.

Apparently putting the ball through the hoop wasn't the most important thing, for the fans fell in love with the little gestures Earvin and Larry displayed. Somehow, the way Johnson smiled made people melt. And with Larry, well, just seeing him in class was so good because he was actually someone you could reach out and touch. He could do so little and be so great. Against Southern Illinois on February 15, Bird saved the game with a blocked shot and the most subtle of plays. Indiana State led by one point with 14 seconds left when Sycamore guard Steve Reed was fouled. His first shot went in, but the second shot rimmed out. Bird went high into the air, and tapped the rebound to Reed, who was fouled again. His first free throw enabled State to escape with a 69–68 win, and all Bird had to do was touch the ball once to make the Sycamore's twenty-fourth win in a row possible.

It's not hard to imagine why folks in Terre Haute and East Lansing lined up outside the stadium as much as 5 hours before game time. It's no coincidence that attendance records were set at both schools this season, and although both teams would be formidable again in the

years to come this was their finest hour. Johnson set his
mind to defense as the Spartans defeated Indiana and
Michigan back-to-back to go 18–5 overall and 10–4 in
league play. Earvin took on the task of shutting down
the Big Ten's leading scorer, 7' Joe Barry Carroll as
Michigan State knocked Purdue out of the conference
race with a 73–67 victory on February 21. The Spartans
were now 11–4 in the Big Ten with one last home game
remaining against Illinois before finishing on the road at
Minnesota and Wisconsin. Indiana State defeated Drake
76–68 to go to 25–0 and set the stage for Bird's final
regular-season home game against Wichita State.

By now, Magic was so much of a celebrity that he
traveled around the state playing games of "Horse" in
front of large crowds. He even challenged his sister
Evelyn to a game back at Everett. But his final curtain
call came on February 24 when he bowed out of Jenison
with a triple double. He scored 21 points, 11 rebounds,
and 11 assists—and all the while insisted he was playing
a supporting role to his senior friend Kelser, who would
soon be graduating. Magic left the fans cheering for
more as, on the first play of the game, he made eye
contact with Kelser before throwing a picturesque alley-
oop lob pass for a slam dunk. Only the thought of this
possibly being Earvin's final home game for Michigan
State could turn the cheers to tears.

Otherwise, the noise was so utterly piercing that it
practically could be heard in and around Indiana. Or
were they making their own noise, for at the same time,
Bird was bidding adieu to his fans in a way only he
could fashion? Talk about a shocking performance; Wichita's State's Shockers were still wondering what it had
been 4 or 5 years later. Bird saved his best for last—a

49-point performance with 19 rebounds that was a story in itself. National television was on hand for the game, and the school put out a souvenir program to honor the occasion. Finally the country had to take notice, and on February 27, 1979, Indiana State was the unanimous choice as the top-ranked team in both wire-service polls.

Michigan State, too, was in the process of making it to the top of the mountain. Earvin scored 21 points on February 28 as the Spartans defeated Minnesota, 76–63, to wrap up at least a share of the conference championship. After all the team had endured, was it finally time for Magic to raise his index finger and not just be leading cheers? Or would the Spartans come up just short? Call it 55 feet short to be exact, for that was the distance of the shot that Wisconsin's Wes Mathews hit right before the final buzzer to give his team an 83–81 upset of Michigan State and force the team to share the conference crown with Iowa. On that same night, Indiana State defeated New Mexico State to win the Missouri Valley Conference post-season tournament championship.

No one could have asked for a better scenario. The big winner during this year would be the basketball fans, for they would get to witness the two greatest college players doing it all. If only CBS television had been along to chronicle this road to the Final Four. Bird paved the way for the Sycamores by scoring 22 and 29 points respectively in NCAA tournament victories over Virginia Tech, 86–69, and Oklahoma, 93–72. Larry was in form he had never been in before as Indiana State moved into a showdown with Arkansas for the Mideast Regional Championship and a shot at the Final Four. The feeling was mutual about how rare this Bird was. "People who have seen you play for the first time in person think you're better than when they saw you on television," was the remark put to Bird during a pregame press conference. "Yeah, they know what they're talking about," he answered without hesitation. He was the best thing on television in leading the Sycamores to a 73–71 win over Arkansas with 31 points, 10 rebounds, and 3 assists. State rode Bird's prowess and a last-second shot by Bobby Heaton to Salt Lake City, Utah, the final destination and sight of the Final Four and NCAA championship game.

And from Motown, Earvin Johnson and his Michigan State teammates came free-wheeling and dealing into Salt Lake City. The Spartans left a lot of devastated coaches and players in their paths, and it was left to Notre Dame coach Digger Phelps, whose team had lost to Magic and company in the NCAA Midwest Regional final, to find just the right words to describe how good Michigan State was: "They're playing better basketball than any team in the country right now."

The Final Four features more hype and hoopla over hoops than any other single college basketball competition in America. But in 1979 the hype and hoopla over Bird and Magic turned the event into the Final Two. The greatest year in college basketball was going to come down to the ultimate game of one-on-one. Bird would get the ball at the top of the key with time running out and the game tied. He'd give Magic a head-fake, spin to his left, and swish a fadeaway in Earvin's face.

Well, it could have happened that way.

Bird did at least that much and more in the process of tearing apart DePaul with 35 points, 16 rebounds, and 9 assists in a 76–74 win in the national semifinal. Apparently the broken thumb he suffered in the Missouri Valley Conference Tournament didn't bother Larry when he went diving over the DePaul bench after a loose ball. Bird hit 16 of 19 shots from the field, and bewildered the Blue Demons with such moves as a behind-the-head pass between 2 defenders. Such a pass went to Heaton who converted it into a 75–74 ISU lead with 36 seconds left. "I don't know how I got that pass to Bobby," Bird said. "The ball got through a lot of hands. Basketball is lucky sometimes. That was luck."

This Final Four afternoon was quite the double feature. In the second performance of the day, Magic put on a tremendous show in leading Michigan State to a 101–67 victory over Pennsylvania in the other semifinal. Earvin stole the show with 29 points, 10 rebounds, and 10 assists and in the process gave national publicity to the concept of triple double. All of which set the stage for the grand finale, and as soon as the afternoon's festivities ended, all attention turned toward Magic and the Bird. How appropriate it was that they would share top billing.

"It seems the whole country is caught up in the Magic Man versus Bird Man matchup," said Spartan coach Heathcote.

Added Johnson: "People kept coming up to me and saying, 'You and Bird—what a show.' I guess it will be. We like to play against the best."

Bird, on other hand, didn't lose sleep over the matter. The morning after the game he was supposed to appear at a breakfast to accept the award as the National Player of the Year, but when coach Bill Hodges went to wake him up at 9 A.M., Bird requested more sack time.

While Bird was a sleeping giant, Michigan State went off to prepare a game plan to stop Indiana State. Johnson played the role of imitating Bird in this pre-championship-game practice, and teammate Terry Donnelly admitted, "There were times we couldn't tell the difference." For the next 24 hours, everyone was talking about who would prevail. Said DePaul coach Ray Meyer, "Michigan State is playing the best basketball in the country." Boys who would be boys went down to the gym and played out the one-on-one. "You be Magic, I'll be Bird" signaled the start of the game, and they ran out of time before they ran out of shots. (Johnson drives baseline, but Bird is there to block his path. Magic fakes a pass, Bird moves and Earvin goes in for the lay-up.)

Well, it could have happened that way.

It *did* happen just like that when, in the second half on the championship duel, Magic drove around his defender, then faked on Bird, who came over to help on defense, in order to clear his path to the hole. Michigan State took a 9–8 lead early in the game and never trailed again. The Spartans used, as Magic said, "a man and a half" to stop Bird, and they held the Sycamore star to 19 points. (That is, if one can be held to 19 points.) Larry had trouble getting his shots off, and when he put up an air ball in the first half it was the beginning of the end for Indiana State. Larry's 19 points were the result of 7-for-21 shooting and he only had 2 assists.

Magic scored 24 in the 75–64 victory, and all 5 of his assists were spectacular. Twice he hooked up with Kelser for alley-oop slam dunks, and he was the heart of the defense that held Bird to more than 11 points below his season average. The Spartans led 37–28 at halftime, but in the first 2 minutes of the second half Magic gave his mates the green light, and the team ran off to as much as a 16-point lead. The Sycamores pulled to within 6 points, 52–46, with 10 minutes to play, but Earvin went back to his bag of tricks. He scored a 3-point play, then a 4-point play, MSU went up by 11 points, and Earvin went over to Kelser and laid a big hug on his buddy. ''I told him, 'You had one heck of a game,' '' Kelser said, ''and he said I was one bad dude.''

But amidst all the celebrating, this ultimate game of one-on-one returned to the place where it had started.

''This is better than Christmas,'' Magic told the horde of reporters. ''It's like all the holidays rolled into one. Oooh, you got to love it.''

Responded Bird: ''Michigan State had a real tough defense, and our team just didn't hit the shots tonight. We still won thirty-three games. Earvin is a great player, but I would like to play him again.''

For now, Earvin was one-up on the Bird, but it wouldn't be long before they would be doing battle again. Their one-to-one relationship was only beginning.

INSTANT REPLAY

Not Just Another Game

LARRY BIRD HAS ALWAYS BEEN PLAYING THE SAME GAME, even if it was with a sponge-rubber ball and a coffee can. But even early in his career, Bird knew nights when it was more than just a game. These were most definitely magic moments, events so out of the ordinary even for Larry, who always gave a little something extra when he sensed the game was becoming extraordinary.

February 25, 1979 was one of those nights, and every one of the 10,220 fans who converged on the Hulman Civic Center in Terre Haute knew as much. Somehow the special occasions were always adorned with the intricacies that captured the spirit of the moment. Bob King, the ISU athletic director, greeted all comers with a letter of commendation for Bird. This, of course, was printed in the souvenir Larry Bird "Collector's Edition Home Finale" program complete with Larry Bird's autograph.

The program also featured a special 8-page supplement efficiently depicting the Bird years, including a game-by-game scoring summary of all of Bird's games for the Sycamores. The collector's part of the program was more than a page and a half of notes and quotes from those who'd watched him do his thing. Said Larry Gillman, then-coach at East Carolina, "Bird is the best player in the country without the basketball. And we all know what he can do with the basketball." The best of the lot may have been Jerry Lyne, the Loyola of Chicago basketball coach, who said, "This Larry Bird—you just gotta see him to believe him."

The opponent was an unsuspecting team from Wichita State, but what could be expected from the Shockers whose leading scorer that season was known as Lynbert "Cheese" Johnson? National television was there in the form of NBC for this Sunday afternoon when America would get to see Larry Bird for the first time. It was only appropriate that this would be Bird's final regular-season home game.

So what did Larry do? The first 7 minutes of the game he didn't make a shot, and he threw the ball away a couple of times. Thousands of folks had waited outside the Hulman Center for hours in a heavy snowstorm just to get in to see the game. Could Bird be giving them the cold shoulder? Yet 30 minutes later Hulman would be the hottest place in the country as Bird exited to a relentless standing ovation after scoring 49 points, his most ever as a collegian.

Carl Jones of the Terre Haute *Star* seemed almost prophetic with his contribution to the souvenir program: "Just about the time you think you've seen it all from Larry Bird, he reaches into his bag of tricks and pulls out a few more goodies."

The Sycamores 109–84 victory finished off a 26–0 season and was more or less a big party to celebrate. When Bird finally got hot he made 17 of his last 21 shots and overall he was 18 for 28 in 38 minutes of playing time. He left the fans with a vintage Bird flurry. The score was 52–50 4 minutes into the second half, when Indiana State put together a 17–2 run to blow open the game.

Bird fueled the run with 9 straight points. He stopped and popped from the top of the key, then swished a shot from the corner. He hit the weak-side board to follow up a miss by Carl Nicks and turned the extra effort into a 3-point play. Another offensive rebound turned into another Bird hoop, and Indiana State led 69–52.

With 2½ minutes remaining, Sycamore coach Bill Hodges was on the verge of taking Bird out of the game. Assistant coach Mel Daniels, however said, ''Hey, he's got forty-five. I'd sure like to see him get a couple more buckets.'' Larry calmly hit 2 free throws, then bid farewell for the moment to the fans with a high-arcing, fall-away jump shot from 15 feet that hit nothing but net. Bird had moved the crowd so much that as he left the court for good, the fans burst out into a ringing chorus of *Amen*.

Bird had answered all prayers for the moment, and his extra effort netted him a deserving reward. By the time he would wake up the next day, Indiana State would be the unanimous choice as the top-ranked team in the nation. For now, he could sit back in a whirlpool bath and enjoy what was really important in life. This was just another game.

INSTANT REPLAY
Horse Play

EARVIN JOHNSON NEVER HESITATED TO GO OUT OF HIS way to give a little something extra, so when he put on a show he wanted it to be memorable. There were many nights when he did it his way and seemed as if he were just horsing around with his opponents. These were the times Earvin loved so much, the moments when he palmed the world like a basketball and did the stuffs only he could do.

Actually, the best of times for Earvin was when someone would put a jumper—and a challenge to go with it—right in his face. Johnson was never the type to rise to such an occasion; he always rose above it. Perhaps the way he rose to the top of his game in leading Michigan State from a 5–4 start in the 1988 Big Ten season to a share of the conference championships best illustrates this attribute. Then again, Magic had a slightly eccentric way of showing off his best shots.

Perhaps the best of those times were left on the Main Street playground. Another player hadn't yet learned, so Earvin had to beat him in one last pickup game or one-on-one to take what was left of his money. Sometimes Earvin didn't need to go that far, and instead blew away the challenger in a simple game of Horse, the game in which one player makes a shot and the opponent must duplicate the shot with the same style and flair. The one who misses the shot then receives the letter H, then O, and so on until 5 misses to spell out H-O-R-S-E. Whoever spells out HORSE first loses.

During that championship season of 1979 Earvin returned to his roots to give the hometown folks a moment to remember. The stage was set at Everett High School where Magic would again go face to face with a familiar foe. But this was a player who knew how to get to Earvin, who "knew where he lives," as they say on the playground. This was Evelyn Johnson, Magic's little sister, who was about to show her brother what this game's like when it's really great.

Evelyn was the finest schoolgirl ever to play at Everett, and every bit the player Earvin was. In 3 years at Everett she scored 1,762 points with a senior-year average of 35 per game. In that senior season she scored 804 points, which was one less than Earvin, who played more games. Her 58% shooting placed Everett in the Class A semifinals in the state basketball tournament in 1979.

Evelyn had been hooping with the boys ever since fifth grade. She used to follow Earvin to the schoolyard where she watched and learned. Eventually she got into some of those legendary pickup games. And the boys made her pay.

"These guys always played for money and so did she," Earvin said. "But I'll tell you, the talent is there. The thing I tell here about is upstairs—her brain. I tell her to be smart."

So together, the highest-scoring brother-sister act in Michigan high school history went at it for old time's sake, fun, and the benefit of the fans. But no money; this was a free show. HORSE until someone goes down shooting, or at least best-of-3 games. The smart money, though, was on Evelyn, who had a great touch and range with her jumper all the way out to the locker room. She had already gunned down Jay Vincent, Earvin's good friend and Michigan State teammate, in a similar competition.

Evelyn flaunted her range to start the game, and Earvin came up empty. Then he put one back in her face to tie up the first game at H. Boom! Evelyn swished twin 22-foot jumpers to send Earvin to H-O-R. But this was when Magic was at his best, and with a series of nifty bank and scoop shots he came back to take the first game. Still, Evelyn came within one letter of defeating her big brother.

There would be no denying her in game 2. Evelyn hit from long distance to put Earvin down a letter. The Magic Man went cold. Body English couldn't even bail him out. He had H-O-R. He rallied. He lost.

Suddenly, Earvin started to take the game seriously, and that made Earvin Sr., who was watching on the sidelines, just a little nervous. Magic went up by 2 letters, but Evelyn turned it on to put her brother down to one last letter. So Earvin did what he did best. He smiled. "I got you right where I want you," he said.

"I'm gonna get you yet." Earvin's best stuff tied the game. Next letter loses. Earvin suffered through a couple of misses, yelled, "Pressure's on," and hit a shot from the corner. Evelyn came up empty. Game, set, match to Earvin. Payment came in the form of a hug and a kiss.

4

Don't Touch That Dial

THIS PARTICULAR MIDWINTER SUNDAY WAS FILLED WITH too much of the same old stuff for comfort. The Celtics were losing again to some Supersonics or Trailblazers or Cavaliers, so how could the average couch potato kick back into a Lazy-Boy, and bear to watch? It had all been seen before, even without the benefit of instant replay. Hit the remote control. See if ESPN offers something more stimulating like Australian Rules Football or Championship Power Boat Racing. *Almost Anything Goes* at this point, just as long as it isn't anything like the NBA. Perhaps things will be better next Sunday and the telecast of the NBA Game of the Week will be blacked out locally.

Welcome to 1979, the Dark Ages of the NBA, when the pro game seemed to be mired in a twilight zone. There used to be a shining star up, up, and away, but now darkness had set in on the edge of town. The dawning of the age of desperation was also the time when the once star-studded National Basketball Association was losing its luster. Let network television be the judge; commercials were quickly becoming the best part of the NBA on CBS. Some said in not so many words that the NBA was downright dull. How long before the entire entity would fade to black?

How could professional basketball have become such a sight for sore eyes? Too many blowouts, too many highlights of another slam dunk, too many nights of the same old thing. When was the last time the Boston Celtics finished in last place? The 1978–79 season, when the NBA was looking straight down one big black hole. Larry Bird summed up the whole ordeal when he visited the Garden after his senior season at Indiana State to watch the Celtics play. "I can see why people don't like to watch pro basketball," he commented. "I don't like to watch it either. It's not exciting."

It was a time to conjure up all the available foresight in order to see the light at the end of the tunnel, and to remember it's always darkest before the dawn. (1979 *was* the NBA's darkest hour.) Then, in a flash, the NBA was blinded by the light. Here were Larry Bird and Magic Johnson bursting on the scene like a supernova. Or was that merely the reflection of Magic's smile that shed a guiding light, a beacon showing that better times lay ahead? No matter how thick the night, Magic and the Bird came on like a ray of sunshine. Tomorrow would definitely be a brighter day for the NBA.

The bright lights were shining on Bird and Johnson the moment they became members of the NBA, and if nothing else both Larry and Earvin made sure there was never a dull moment. As soon as they turned on the juice, it was time to run, gun, and have fun. Lighting it up took on a whole new meaning. Fans could once again raise their glasses to toast professional basketball.

In the NBA it isn't always easy to figure how a star is born. On the dark side in the spring of 1979, the Boston Celtics and the Los Angeles Lakers weren't exactly the vibrant professional franchises that were the foundation of the National Basketball Association. the Celtics finished with a 29–53 record, the worst in franchise history since their 32–50 mark the year before. The Lakers went 47–35, but that was with Kareem Abdul-Jabbar, who was just 32 years old, a 10-year veteran, and in the prime of his tremendous NBA life. Fans weren't exactly flocking to the Forum in L.A. or the Boston Garden, and after the 1979 season ended each club was sold. Basketball's version of the big bang theory seemed the only plausible solution. It was time for the NBA to be born again, and it was left to a couple of mere babes on the hardwood to breathe life back into the league. Magic was a walking, talking, grinning burst of energy, the kind of guy who jumped up and down after every basket. And Bird was a player who could make you feel young again. Word around Boston was that Bird was just like the players from the old Celtics that fathers had been telling their sons stories about. Magic and Bird weren't just drafted in the league; they made a grand entrance somewhere along the line of a coronation.

Bird was drafted after his junior season at Indiana State, although at that point he wasn't even interested in the pro game. Players who want to forego remaining college eligibility to become professional apply with the league for what is known as hardship status. Bird made no such declaration. In fact, Wilt Chamberlain was perhaps the only other more prominent player to be drafted by a professional team before college graduation. Back then, the NBA didn't even allow underclassmen to be drafted. But Boston general manager Red Auerbach wanted to make sure to get the rights to Bird, even though he knew it might mean waiting another year before he could play in the NBA.

All of which prevented the opportunity for the 1979 NBA draft to come down to making a decision between Magic and Bird. Who would you choose? Magic went to the Lakers, who had the first pick, and the deal was done by the end of May, a month or so before the actual draft was to take place.

It wasn't quite that simple. Magic had problems with his agent, Georgia attorney Jack Manton, and a difference of opinion let to a parting of ways. So Magic smiled and looked across the bargaining table at the Lakers' new owner, Dr. Jerry Buss. Someone made someone an offer that couldn't be refused, and it was a deal. Some reports indicated that Magic would receive $300,000 a year for 4 years and another 100,000 as a signing bonus. Others say that the deal was bit more lucrative and included real estate and deferred money. The bottom line is that the man was worth the investment.

Money, as you will see, was not the most important thing to Larry. When it came to the matter of choosing an agent, Bird went to play softball. The people of Terre Haute, Indiana, made sure Larry was well-cared-for. A committee of the city's leading citizens interviewed 60 or more perspective agents, and decided on Boston attorney Bob Woolf, who represented John Havlicek (one of the infamous old Celtic players).

Getting Bird signed with Boston, however, was quite another story. On April 6, 1979, Bird made his first visit to Boston and the Garden. Money was no object on this expedition, and Woolf put Larry and Dinah Mattingly up at the posh Parker House, one of Boston's finer hotels. Bird was one of 7,831 fans who saw the Celtics lose their seventh game in a row on a night so bland that Bird wore an obtrusive tan sports shirt and went largely unnoticed. He left before the end of the game. (Years later, Woolf showed a hotel bill that had nothing more than the room charge and tax on it. There was no room service, no long-distance telephone calls, no luxuries whatsoever.)

Money, though, was the problem. Boston had to sign Bird before the 1979 draft or the club would lose the rights to its future. Woolf came to the Celtics with an offer of a million a year, and Auerbach choked. He offered half that much and reasoned, "It's been proven a cornerman can't dominate the game. A big man, occasionally even a guard. But one man playing a corner can't turn a franchise around."

Auerbach and all of Boston couldn't be convinced that Bird was worth so much. Supposedly the NBA wasn't worth that much, as an editorial in the Boston *Globe* suggested: "Pro basketball had achieved the ultimate and the ultimate appears to have limited appeal." Woolf wouldn't budge either. His children were threatened in school. He got lost in nearby Worcester, and when he stopped to ask directions he was told, "Not unless you promise to sign Bird." No lies told; no promises broken.

But Bird stood by Woolf, the man he'd chosen to represent him over another agent because "the other man was too smart for me.'' Finally, on June 9, 1979—another date that will live in infamy—Auerbach met with Woolf in his office. Auerbach walked out. He walked back in. He walked out again. After more than 3 hours the deal was indeed done. Larry signed a 5-year contract for $3.25 million ($650,000 a year), which made him the highest-paid rookie in the history of league.

But the money was no object to Bird. ''If I fail, I fail. I failed classes before. I know the feeling.'' Less than 4 months later, Woolf and Bird were driving back from a visit to the Basketball Hall of Fame in Springfield when Woolf said what the whole town was thinking. ''All I can say is you better be good.'' Bird gave him a wink, and responded, ''I'll knock 'em dead.'' But what, pray tell, if he didn't? Bird just laughed and said, ''Then everybody will say, 'Gee, I don't know what could have happened to him. He sure was good in college.' ''

It is important to consider at this point how good Magic and Bird were when they came into the NBA. There never will be 2 players who could make the ball move as magnificently as they did. It was the dawning of the age of the pass, and Larry and Earvin put the motion into the concept of motion offense. No one will ever pass this way again and no one had before. As *Sports Illustrated* pointed out, ''Earvin (Magic) Johnson and Larry Bird did for the pass what Dr. J and David T. (Thompson) did for the dunk.''

So what did Bird do to make immediate impact on Boston? The day after moving into town he got lost jogging. Magic was considerably more effervescent when he came to town. The rest of the Lakers didn't even call him Magic. "Young Buck" was his nickname, because "there were just rivers of emotion coming out of him," remembered Jerry West, the Lakers' general manager. "He was all over the place, smiling, laughing, jumping up and down after every basket."

The team was in need of such youthful enthusiasm. Attendance had dropped by an average of 4,500 per game in the past 8 years. The club had talent and a major drawing card in Kareem, but what the Lakers needed to make more than a pass at a championship was personality. Johnson gave them more than just personality.

"If it was just personality," George Andrew, who works in publicity at the Forum, said, "they'd probably hire the San Diego Chicken. But he can't go to his left."

The business of basketball caught up with both Larry and Earvin before each played his first pro game. Endorsement offers came their way, and even Magic said, "Now it's a job." Magic made his debut in a Laker uniform that summer in a rookie league game at California State University. He scored 24 points and had 9 assists in 29 minutes, and there were 3,000 Lakers fans on hand to witness the event. Both the Lakers and Celtics could look forward to windfall gains. Boston sold 6,000 season tickets for Bird's rookie season, 3,000 more than the year before. The rest of the teams in the NBA would soon share in the success.

If there was any question as to the impact Magic and the Bird made on the NBA, remember that all the aforementioned incidents happened before either had played a minute of pro ball. Even moving without the ball couldn't free Earvin and Larry from media coverage. In Bird's first days in Boston, when he was out jogging and lost his way home, an enamored fan offered a lift. The incident made the news. The story of his contract negotiations inspired a continuing series in the Boston *Globe*. And over on the other coast, when Magic bought a condominium it made the nightly news.

But to the fans in both cities no news meant Larry or Earvin hadn't done anything. What, after all, were they getting paid for? How about 18 points against Philadelphia, 13 points against Washington, and 36 points and 15 rebounds against the New York Knicks in the first 3 exhibition games? Standard fare for Bird, who looked at such numbers and said, "Well, I know I can't be great right off." Larry was the only new face in the Celtic starting lineup, which had finished the last season with a 29–53 record. Now Boston was 3–0.

Magic was one of 7 new faces among the Lakers, not counting new owner Buss and new coach Jack McKinney. It's tough to come right in and throw those no-look passes off the fast break to someone you'd never met. A lot of noses are broken that way, and a lot of friendships. The team paved the way for Magic by moving spunky Norm Nixon from his role as the playmaker to shooting guard. It was Earvin's show to run. "A lot of times I messed up because I thought somebody would be somewhere they weren't, or because they thought I couldn't see them when they were open. I hit a lot of people in the face at first, and I got a lot of turnovers, but I just worked at it until I got it right."

It didn't take long for Earvin to get it right. In his first 3 exhibition games, the tallest guard in the NBA hit 20 of his first 30 shots from the field. More than that, Earvin super-charged the Lakers and drove them to life in the fast break lane. Even Kareem was diving for loose balls and showing the hustle that belied 10 years of experience. Magic didn't just have the Lakers feeling young again. They were born again.

Opening night was October 12, a night with little infamy. Newspapers across America devoted barely more than a few lines to the occasion; the league was still buried in the bushes. Bird netted some publicity when he scored 14 points and grabbed 10 rebounds as the Celtics beat Houston, 114–106 in front of 15,230 fans in the Garden. But the evening may have been noteworthy only because some fan released a white dove into the arena before the start of the game. Slightly more space was devoted to Bird's 28-point effort in a 139–117 blowout of Cleveland in the second game, but only because he scored 16 of those points in a flurry—7-for-10 shooting from the field.

Magic didn't make headlines until he hurt his knee in the third game of the season and the Lakers suspected that he might be out for up to 6 weeks. Johnson was examined the day after his disaster, and the diagnosis indicated it was just a sprain; the prognosis said he'd be back in 10 days. "The pain went away when I heard that," he said. Already he had been a pain to opponents with 45 points, 12 assists, and 17 rebounds.

How badly off were the Lakers without their point guard? They won 4 in row, which led to a jubilant return for the Magic man on October 30. He came as close to home as he had been this season when the Lakers played the Bulls at the Chicago Stadium. (It had taken on a green and white glow courtesy of all the fans who'd come south from East Lansing.) Magic left them with a rare highlight when he bounced a pass off referee Earl Strom in the opening minutes. But Earl wasn't filling his lane on the fast break, and Magic scored 24 points anyway.

More than 16,000 fans packed the Stadium that night, and the next night 7,012 fans stood in the Brendan Byrne Arena in Piscataway, New Jersey and chanted Bird's name. After he scored 18 points and left the game with 2 minutes to play, the crowd gave Larry an even louder ovation.

In Philadelphia, they packed the Spectrum for Boston's first visit for a different reason. In the pre-season Bird had faced the 76ers' Julius Erving in a low-profile affair. This time it was high style, and the first regular-season meeting of Bird and the Doc. For 8 years they would shadow each other through an epic duel. Testimony to their match-up came in the form of the computer game now bearing their names. Through the years they gave each other their best shots. One time they even hit each other. The season used to end for them with one of them losing in the playoffs to the other.

As soon as Erving went over 2 Celtic defenders for the game-winning lay-up in a 95–94 victory, the Doc came out on top. He scored 37 points and pulled down 10 rebounds. But he didn't make it without a mark on his face. Bird scored 8 points in 2 minutes of the first quarter, forcing Erving to the bench. And then down the stretch, Bird answered Erving's 18-foot fadeaway jumper with a 19-foot back-in-your-face jumper. Erving hit his baseline lay-up to win; Bird missed on his last shot. At the time, Bird knew it's not where you start, it's where you finish.

"I thought I played good defense on him," Bird said, "but he's the best forward in the league. When he's going good, he's hard to stop. I ain't the only forward in the league he's scored on.''

Time for a quick review. Bird was putting the ball in the hoop at a rate of 20 points per game, and attendance in the Garden increased more than 3,000 per game on the average. The place was up to 90% capacity. Earvin, on the other coast, was now simply identified as Magic. Kareem tried to refer to him in public as Earvin, but nobody knew who the big guy was talking about. The Lakers and Celtics were on a run and leading their respective divisions. Leave it to Magic and Larry to put the feeling into words.

"When we get the fast break going and everyone knows where they're supposed to be, that's when we play our best ball,'' said the Bird Man. And Magic added, ''When we start running my confidence starts to rise. That's when I know it's time to deal on some people. When we're rolling and the break is going, I guess it looks like I'm performing magic out there. There are some nights I think I can do anything.''

Magic had just finished scoring a career-high 31 points in a 126–122 victory over Denver on November 13. He had never been more magical as a pro with 8 baskets to spark a game-winning rally. He finished with 10-for-16 shooting from the field in the second half alone and added 8 assists and 6 rebounds.

Was Bird a young rookie or an old pro when he scored 23 points and had 19 rebounds and 10 assists in a 115–111 victory over Detroit? "I'm just playing as hard as I can. I don't consider myself a rookie,'' Bird commented. ''I know I can make it in this league. I've just got to go out and prove it.''

How much more proof would there have to be for

Larry and Earvin to prove their net worth? Bird scored in double figures in his first 19 games, including one triple double. But it was also the little things that provided the big dividends. Bird hit a 3-point shot at the third-quarter buzzer of a game against New Jersey on November 21 that sparked the Celtics to a 111–103 victory. The shot put the Celtics ahead 82–81 for the first time in the game, "and it was like they gave him a touch of a wand," said Eddie Jordan of the Nets. "It was magic. Everything went for them after that." Magic scored 23 points in a 116–103 win over Milwaukee, but it was his 8 points sparking a 18–0 fourth-quarter Laker run that made the difference. By December 9, when Bird scored a career-high 32 points against Cleveland, the Celtics were at 21–7 and in first place in the Atlantic Division of the Eastern Conference while the Lakers were 20–10 and leading the Pacific Division of the Western Conference.

Coaches, opposing players, and members of the media were beginning to run off at the mouth over what Magic and Bird had accomplished in the first 2 months of the season. They were all talking about this concept of a run as, for example, "the Lakers used a 16–2 third-quarter run to turn the game into a blowout." The run had become an inherent part of both the Celtics and the Lakers. Magic would make a steal and hit Jammal Wilkes with a half-court bounce pass for a lay-up, which ignited the team to play defense that much harder the next time down. Kareem would block a shot, Magic would pick up the loose ball, and get the club off and running. It compounds. The more to the run the more intense it gets. Bird would come down the left side, break to the middle of 2 defenders, and flip a behind-the-back pass to Gerald Henderson for a lay-up. Henderson then makes a steal and sets up Bird and suddenly you come back from getting popcorn and the Celtics have turned a 6-point deficit into a 12-point lead. If this is the Knicks or the Nets or the Bullets they have just been run out of the gym.

What made the run so wonderful was that one player— usually Magic or Bird—wound up hitting for a bunch of points in a row. Like when Bird scored 11 of his 24 points in a decisive second-quarter run to help the Celtics blow out the Sixers, 112–89, on December 19 in the Garden. Bird and Cedric Maxwell combined to score 16 of the 21 points in a third-quarter run, leading Boston to a 133–114 win over San Antonio on December 22. That was the latest win in a 7-game run for the Celtics.

In Hollywood and on Broadway, "run" is also a frequent modifier to describe the extended success of a production. If that was the case, then what was happening in the NBA was most definitely show time. Especially in Inglewood, California, on December 29, 1979, when the Celtics came to the Forum to meet the Lakers for the first of 2 games in this regular season. This was the first meeting since March, and a funny thing happened to Magic and Bird on the way to the Forum. All the pre-game hype centered on the 2 rookies. Magic, they pointed out, was the only Laker to be featured in a full-page advertisement in the game program. In L.A., they were using his smile to sell soda pop on billboards. Bird was accorded similar face time, yet called all the hype "stupid."

Too bad the game was far from a 4-star production. Magic prevailed again, and more easily this time. The Magic Man scored 23 points, had 8 rebounds and 6 assists, and no wonder he called it a "special game." The Celtics called it their worst game of the season. It was probably special only because the crowd reached a capacity of 17,505, the first sellout of a regular season game in the Forum since March 12, 1978 (and only the fifth since the start of the 1977–78 season).

What made the game memorable was a series of events late in the fourth quarter, when Boston was trailing by 15 points. Magic came driving through the lane all bright-eyed and smiling. He crashed into Bird, and this was no laughing matter. There were no smiles. "He just looked at me and I looked at him," Bird said. "I don't go out and eat with him. I just know him on the basketball floor and that's it. If he thinks he's going to drive the lane and I'm going to lay down, he's crazy."

The thing was, though, in the end Bird had no hard feelings. He knew he and Magic were the center of attention because it was vital to the league. It was not as if they had to carry everything on their shoulders, but, as Bird said, the NBA put considerable weight on Magic and himself because "they got to. They ain't got nobody they can lean on." They were the leading men, which is why CBS scheduled the second Lakers-Celtics meeting on January 13, 1980 for the season premiere of the NBA on CBS. Bird and the Celtics were booked into the first 3 Sundays of the NBA on CBS.

When all the world was watching, Earvin and Larry were a bust. The Celtics closed down the magic act as Johnson scored but one point. Bird had 14 points, far below his season standard. Only a 100–98 comeback win by L.A. with Kareem scoring 31 kept the NBA from being canceled on CBS.

Where the ratings mattered most, the Celtics were in first place one-half game ahead of Philly, while the second-place Lakers were trailing Seattle by a half-game. Bird scored a pro-high 36 points on January 27 in a 131–108 rout of the San Diego Clippers. Then as January came to a close, Larry convinced all remaining doubters he had that star quality.

This was vintage Bird in a 119–103 win over Washington. During a 5-minute third-quarter run Bird scored 10 of his 24 points in a row. He spotted up from the 3-point line and swished a fallaway "J." The he pulled up and downed a another 3. He set up center Rick Robey for a lay-up with a one-touch pass. Bird fed Robey for another lay-up. By the end of the run, Boston outscored Washington 40–20 in the third period, when Bird also had 7 rebounds and 5 assists.

The NBA's annual star search spotlighted Earvin and Larry to be part of the thirtieth annual All-Star Game in Washington. Magic had 12 points and 2 steals; Bird scored 7 points and had 7 assists as Bird's team—the East—beat Magic and the rest of the best of the West, 144–136. This, however, was a ratings game, and the NBA had outscored the college basketball Game of the Week telecast by a count of 8.5 to 5.3. That's a no-contest in the ratings game. As Chicago *Tribune* columnist Bob Verdi wrote in his review of the All-Star Game, "With a new superstar in Boston and Los Angeles, Larry Bird and Earvin Magic Johnson, interest is high again."

Magic and Bird ran out the regular season on top. Bird posted a first-year high of 45 points against Phoenix on February 13 and finished the season with an average of 21.3 points per game. He also contributed

more than 10 rebounds and 4 assists per game, numbers
which made him the unanimous choice as Rookie of the
Year. Magic was the second-best rookie with an 18
points-per-game average to go with 7 rebounds and 7
assists. Boston won the Atlantic Division title with a
61-21 record, 2 games ahead of the Sixers and 22
games ahead of third-place Washington. The Lakers
won the Pacific Division with a 60-22 mark, 4 games
better than defending champion Seattle. Such records
were the top 2 in the NBA that season.

All of which meant a week's vacation for Magic and
the Bird and the Lakers and the Celtics. In the everyone-
is-included NBA playoffs, the winner of each division
skips past the first round. Those 4 teams waited a week
while the other 8 went about narrowing themselves
down to 4.

In any event, a week off didn't seem to matter much;
Magic had a triple double—13 points, 16 assists, 12
rebounds—in his playoff debut, a 119–110 win over
Phoenix. The next night, Johnson hit 2 free throws to
force overtime when the Lakers finally edged the Suns,
131–118. In the third game of the series, Earvin's
clutch steal enabled the Lakers to run off with a 108–105
victory. And then a week after this best-of-7 Western
Conference semifinal series began, Magic closed it out
with 11 assists in a 126–101 L.A. rout. Magic was in
the process of averaging a triple double for the entire
playoffs, so it was no surprise that that Suns were no
match for him.

In one of the Eastern Conference semifinal games,
the Houston Rockets found themselves equally over-
matched. In the first game Bird flaunted a 13-point
flurry in the second quarter and the Celtics rolled to a

119–101 win. What was scary about the victory was that Houston shut down Bird in the second half and held him to 2 points, although Boston still won by 18 points. That was pretty much as close as the Rockets could get. Game 2 went to Boston, 95–75, and game 3 ended with the Celtics on top, 100–81. Bird scored 34 points in game 4 as Boston swept the series with a 138–121 triumph.

This was getting exciting. Bird and the Celtics were matched up against Dr. J and the Sixers in the Eastern Conference finals while the Lakers had a showdown with Seattle. Larry and Earvin were on a collision course that would cross paths in the NBA championship series. This had the makings for a rerun that would be a major television event. Surely the roots of the success pro basketball has enjoyed over the era of the 1980s can be traced back to this playoff period.

First, however, was the matter of these mini-series. Boston vs. Philly was the more glamorous of the conference championship matchups. The Sixers were on the verge of becoming the league's most dominant team, but the Celtics were still the most dominant team in the history of the league. Yet somehow this series transcended team play to focus on the battle of the Bird and the Doc. Perhaps Bird was wrapped up in this subplot; moments before the start of the first game, he was standing in a corner all alone with a blank stare fixed on his face. Teammate Rick Robey inquired as to what was wrong. "Nothing," said Bird calmly. "I'm just practicing up my defense for Dr. J."

The first round went to Erving on points, 29 to 27 for Bird, which sparked Philadelphia to a 96–93 victory. Bird fueled a run with 12 consecutive points in the fourth quarter, but the Doc hit 10 in a row during a third-quarter run, which proved to be decisive. Julius seemed to leave Larry staggering when he burned his rookie counterpart 3 straight times in the early part of game 2. Bird came back to score 15 of the team's next 21 points and he finished that first half with 21 points. Bird put some of the Doc's own stuff back in his face to start the second half and ended with 31 points in the 96–90 Celtic victory.

Everything was falling into place for the networks. Magic even helped thicken the plot. He hurt his arm in the last game against Phoenix, and didn't practice in the days leading up to the first game against Seattle. But as long he had his legs under him, the Lakers were running. A 108–107 loss in the first game didn't slow Los Angeles down. It was just a momentary setback.

In the playoffs, greatness comes from being in the right place at the right time. Earvin Johnson never did anything spectacular without the right amount of pageantry. In game 2, he made sure Jack Nicholson, Walter Matthau, Valerie Perrine, and the rest of the stars were watching when he snuck up behind the Sonic's Fred Brown and picked the ball right out of his pocket. The steal protected the Lakers' 99–94 lead and sent them on their way to a 108–99 win. Magic was the star of stars with 19 points, 9 assists, and 6 steals.

It wasn't long before Magic would steal the entire series from Seattle. After a 104–100 win in game 3, game 4 brought out the best in the Magic Man. Seattle had as much as a 21-point lead in the first half, but that was no match for the ultimate Laker run. A 24–0 spurt in the third quarter brought the team back to a 73–72 lead, and an 11–0 fourth-quarter stretch sealed the victory. Magic wasn't even breathing heavily despite 15 points, 13 rebounds, and 6 assists. In this victory his defense had fueled the Laker runs. He could do it all—could he do anymore?

The Western Conference finals ended with an anticlimactic 11–105 Laker victory. It took only 5 games, and so Los Angeles waited for its next victim. Magic was smiling when the series ended. It was a year and a month after he and Larry had squared off for the NCAA title, and here they were on the verge of playing for the Big Cake.

But Magic had the last laugh. Bird was tremendous in game 3 of the Eastern conference finals. He had 22 points, including a 3-point shot in the fourth quarter which had cut a one-time, 14-point Sixer lead to 99–97 with 39 seconds left. Boston got the ball back, but the ball never got to Bird to take a final shot to tie the game. Larry had come up short in a big way. He scored 80 points in the first 3 games of the series, but he had just 19 points on 6-of-16 shooting in a 102–90 loss in game 4. And the bottom line for the final game of the season for Bird was 12 points on 5-of-19 shooting.

Earvin could smile approvingly because he had gone one-up on Bird once again. He closed out the Seattle series with a 20-point, 10-rebound, 10-assist performance and was on his way to averaging a triple double for all the playoffs. But the grinning would have to wait until the winning was finished.

With 4:21 left in the third quarter of the first game of the NBA finals, the Lakers threatened to run Philadelphia right out of the playoffs. The Lakers broke a 53-all tie with 12 straight points as Magic had the club running and dunking. He scored 16 points, 10 aasists, and

9 rebounds in the 109–102 Laker victory—and his best was yet to come. The Sixers came back in game 2 to tie the series with a 107–104 victory and a performance so inconsequential the report didn't even make headlines in the papers back East.

But the series was coming back East after the first 2 games in Los Angeles. Magic proved to be the toast of both coasts with 16 points and 11 rebounds in a 111–101 victory in game 3, and he was still saving his best for last. The Sixers squeaked by for a 105–102 victory in game 4 to tie the series at 2 games apiece. Now it was the best 2 of the remaining 3 for the title.

Yet basketball fans collectively gasped when Kareem Abdul-Jabbar went down with an ankle injury in the fifth game. He had scored, rebounded, and intimidated enough for the Lakers to triumph 108–103 and a 3–2 series lead, but the big fella would be lost for the next game.

That only meant that center stage belonged to Earvin, who stepped into fill Kareem's shoes and thereby played center for the first time since high school. Those were some big feet Magic showed, but he wasn't about to put his foot in his mouth. Sitting at home watching Magic go up after the opening tip was mesmerizing. It was the kind of game where at the end of the first quarter, you just had to call up your best friend and tell him to turn on the game. You gotta see this; you're not gonna believe it. Magic scored 42 points and willed the Lakers to a 123–107 victory for the title.

For Earvin, the entire season had seemed like an instant replay. A little more than a year later, he'd stand with a champagne bottle in hand, toasting the greatest team in the land. ''The NCAA was great, but this is greater,'' he said.

The Magic Man continued to crack wise all over the championship locker room; CBS captured every moment. Earvin even stepped right up to the microphone and exchanged words with Brent Musburger. The season would last as long as Johnson wanted to talk, or until the film ran out. Finally the season faded to black, but after what Magic and the Bird had done for the NBA, fans could hardly wait until they turned it on again.

INSTANT REPLAY
Magic Goes Big Time

THIS WAS THE START OF SOMETHING BIG, SO MAGIC JOHNSON merely giggled. He always laughs when despair was in his face. The biggest game of the 1980 season was about to begin, and Magic, as usual, was the center of attention. The Los Angles Lakers came to Philadelphia for the sixth game of the NBA finals with a 3–2 lead in the best-of-7 series. As the big fella, Kareem Abdul-Jabbar, told his teammates, "We got three. We only need one more now." This promised to be a really big show.

But the plot took a definite twist. Actually, it was Kareem's ankle that twisted, so badly during the second half of game 5 that he did not even accompany the team to Philadelphia. Kareem stayed home in bed, and Magic was in Philadelphia grinning over the thought of taking the big guy's place at center for game 6. This was his big chance.

Part of the popular culture of basketball is the karma of being the big man on the team. It's an honor accorded to the biggest and the best, the one who's always the first pick in any game, pickup or otherwise. "I'll take my big man here," says the captain. Or simply, "C'mon, big man, you're with me." At 7'2", Kareem is the best of the biggest; he is simply known as the "big fella." He is so well-respected that the rest of the Lakers concede him the seat on the aisle in the first row on the left of every plane trip. Such a seat is more like a throne, and it also has the most leg room.

But on flight 707 to Philadelphia on May 16, 1980, 6'8" Earvin Johnson occupied the first seat on the aisle in the first row on the left. For the first time since he played at Everett High School, Johnson was going to be the post man. The big man; the big guy. He was going to be Kareem for a day.

In the 123–107 Los Angeles victory over the Sixers, which sealed the league title, Earvin played all 5 positions and made it look as if he were doing it at the same time. Magic hit sky hooks, jump shots, lay-ups off the drive, and scored a career-high 42 points. He had 15 rebounds, 7 assists, 3 steals, and even a blocked shot. He once again was named Most Valuable Player of the championship series. Earvin was bigger than life.

"Magic was outstanding, unreal," said Julius Erving, the glorious Dr. who couldn't believe this dose of magic from Earvin.

Added Lakers' coach Paul Westhead: "Magic thinks every season goes like this. You play some games, win the title, and get named MVP."

Perhaps the only thing that went wrong for Johnson all night was that he lost the opening tip to the Sixers'

Caldwell Jones. Afterwards, this was no laughing matter. In the first half, he was a point guard from the high post as he threw an over-the-shoulder pass to Michael Cooper for a lay-up. He took it coast to coast and pulled up to hit a jump shot. He drove by Erving for another hoop, then he tried to put one in the face of Philadelphia's mammoth center Darryl Dawkins.

"I wanted to dunk it for Kareem," said Earvin, who eventually double pumped and scooped the ball in off the glass, "but I saw Dawkins coming, and I thought I better change to something a little more magical."

The Lakers were given little chance of winning without Kareem, but Magic was doing fine as the little big man. He hit 7 of 12 shots from the field in the first half and helped the Lakers go from a 52–44 deficit to a 60–60 tie at the half. In the second half, Magic hit another 7 of 11 from the floor and also added 14-for-14 from the foul line. Magic pushed the Lakers in the second half, and the club turned it into show time with a 14–0 run to start the third quarter. Magic did it all from everywhere, playing center on offense, forward on defense, and handling the ball whenever he could get his hands on the rock. He said he was tired down the stretch, but he also scored 9 points in the final 2:22.

"Well, I played a little center, a little forward, some guard. I tried to think up a name for it."

It was simply magic, and it brought the Lakers their first NBA championship since 1972. They were not exactly prepared to win the championship here and now. They didn't even bring any champagne with them to Philadelphia. But once that matter was cleared up, it was party time. Then it was show time once again as Magic jumped in front of Brent Musburger, grabbed the microphone, and made a toast from the team into the television cameras.

Kareem had trouble watching the game, and at halftime he turned down the volume because he couldn't bear to listen. But now he saw that Magic was talking to him on national television, so he turned up the volume.

"Big fella, I did it for you," said the Magic Man. "We know you're hurting, but we want you to get up and dance tonight."

Kareem could then celebrate the performance by his Magic Man as much as the NBA championship. "Some things are fate," said the big fella. "I was meant to be here and Earvin was meant to be there. He reminded me of Oscar Robertson, one man playing against boys. Except that Earvin was just one boy playing against men."

To think Earvin was still a kid at 20 and had already won the NBA championship. He had definitely gone Big Time.

5

A Whole New Ball Game

HERE WAS THE WHOLE BALLGAME DOWN TO ONE LAST shot. With 30 seconds left and a one-point deficit at hand, what would Paul Westhead or Bill Fitch do in this situation? Having used a 28–8 fourth-quarter run to come from as much as 20 points down since the start of the fourth quarter, the fast break would seem to be a viable alternative, but now time was standing still. More than a 19-game winning streak was on the line; this was a do-or-die shot. Wilt and Russell, where are you now?

Clearly, the only choice is to go to your big guy, the man in the pivot. Let him post up and do what he does best. Give him the rock and watch him turn his back to the defense and power to the hole. Better yet, he can put up a sweeping hook over all outstretched arms or turn around and shoot the base line J. It's the best-contrived game-winning strategy since the Hickory Huskers ran the "Picket Fence."

Perhaps in an earlier era that would have been the way to go, because back then there was no such thing as weakside help defense to double- and triple-team the ball and foil such plans. But in the 1981 or 1982 NBA playoffs you're just one very big hoop away from winning it all. Kareem and the Chief are double-teamed in the pivot, so if you're Westhead or Fitch or anybody else who knows a little something about the game you give it to Magic or the Bird and let him back the entire defense in toward the hole.

What you now have is a truly pivotal player. Magic glances back over his shoulder and looks for the passing lane. Larry has a gleam in his eyes because he can tell that the other team is certain he's going to turn around and launch a long-distance J. But then it all comes to pass; an over-the-shoulder bullet to Jammal Wilkes or Cornbread Maxwell knocking on the back door. A great pass that wins the game. What a good idea!

Or there's the shot: Magic sweeping across the lane to swish the running baby hook shot, or Bird turning on his right foot and canning the fadeaway 3-point shot. Suddenly, it's a whole new ballgame. Earvin and Larry have found this way to win by moving the basketball or moving without the basketball. The gurus of the game—Dick Vitale included—called this *court awareness*, this matter of giving Johnson and Bird the ball and letting them do what they do best. Nobody does it better.

A look back on what Magic and Bird accomplished during the years 1981–1983 seemed to bring a whole new meaning to the game. Once again it was fashionable to be a teammate, but no one was the teammate quite like Bird or Johnson. Looking back, it was probably the era of Kareem, Dr. J, and Moses, the big guys who were the NBA's Most Valuable Players during those years.

But beyond that, Magic and Bird began to find their own roles in the annals of basketball. If the game was indeed a way of life, then Earvin and Larry ere on the verge of becoming larger than life. In 1981 the Celtics beat the Houston Rockets for the NBA championship, and the following year the Lakers once again topped the Philadelphia 76ers in the finals. In 1983, Philly finally won a title of its own by beating the Lakers, but since Magic and Larry came into the league, the Sixers, the Rockets, the Lakers, the Celtics, and the Detroit Pistons would play for the NBA championship and no one else through 1988. The November 9, 1981, cover of *Sports Illustrated* beamed under a picture of the Bird: "The NBA's Best All-Around Player." A similar basketball preview article in the *New York Times* that year headlined: "Magic: Second to None." Was it no coincidence they were also among the most highly paid players in the game?

Season by season Larry and Earvin were proving themselves to be 2 of a kind. Magic was a guard who had a flare for the pass, yet he defended and rebounded like a forward or a center. Johnson showed that knack to know where a teammate was without looking, just like Larry. Larry was a forward who had a flare for the pass and defended and rebounded like a center. He handled the ball like a guard, like Magic.

As Jack and Nahmie have been discussing for some time, if you had to pick one player—past or present—with whom to start a basketball franchise, who would be that player?

As Dave Cowens, a great Celtic big guy himself and

a teammate of Bird's, said prior to the start of the 1981–82 season, "If I were starting a basketball team, I'd look for a great center, but if I couldn't find a great one, I'd take Larry Bird. No one playing the game today can do as many different things on a court as well as Larry Bird."

Dick Motta, then the coach of the Dallas Mavericks, had just seen Magic score 32 points in his hundredth or so professional game and said, "He might be the best I've ever seen. The only ones better than him may be Jabbar, Wilt, and Russell, and that's only because they are taller than him."

A little more than a year into the NBA and Magic and Bird already stood out in the crowd. It wasn't long before Magic had to tint the windows of his Mercedes so as not to be a traffic hazard. He hurt his knee early in that season, and the crowd followed him everywhere he went as he worked his way back.

As the 1980–81 season was about to begin, every seat in the Boston Garden was sold, even those with obstructed views. And what was about to transpire was something that just couldn't be missed: the explosion of fast-break basketball, when nobody did it better than the Lakers and the Celtics. The ball moved up the floor and into the basket seemingly without touching the floor. If the 1980 season was just a preview, then basketball was going to become a commodity that would keep people in their seats. As Magic said, the whole idea of the whole new ballgame was to "make everybody have fun, to make people happy." And during the course of the next 3 seasons Bird and Johnson went on to provide a preview of just how much fun the NBA could be.

*   *   *

The Lakers were having some fun when the 1980–81 season started. In front of 17,481 fans in Reunion Arena, home of the newest NBA team, the Dallas Mavericks, Magic showed them what pro ball was all about with a flashy 32 points on November 7. A week prior to that the Magic Man had a typical game: 29 points, 10 assists, one especially spectacular on a half-court bounce pass to L.A. forward Jim Chones who was even more startled to see the ball get to him than were the thousands of San Diego fans watching Magic lead the Lakers to a 131–101 rout. Los Angeles was off to a 5–0 start, the best since the team had moved from Minneapolis to California 21 years before.

Across the country, fans were dishing out high-fives just as readily. After watching Bird soar as a rookie, some people were still a bit skeptical. What more could Larry do for the team? One month into the season Bird put up and shut them up. On November 18, the Celtics were battling the Chicago Bulls down to the wire. But in a fourth-quarter flurry, Larry pulled down 8 of his 13 rebounds, then scored 4 points in the final 3 minutes of a 113–112 victory. The next night, Bird scored 19 points and hauled in 18 rebounds in a 103–91 triumph over Indiana.

A little more than one full season into their professional careers, Larry and Earvin put themselves into quite a prominent position. When the victory was there for the taking, forget getting the ball to the big guy and give it to the go-to guy. Tom Heinsohn, former big guy and Celtics coach turned color commentator for the NBA on CBS, watched Boston give it to Bird again and again in the midst of a fourth-quarter run and called him the "go-to guy," the guy the coach would give the ball as if to say, "Go ahead and get us back in the game."

Like when Magic would high-step into overdrive as he led the Lakers on another fast break and another run-from-behind win? The last 5 minutes of the fourth quarter of any game had taken on a new luster. It was a matter of move it or lose it. Even 20-point deficits for the Lakers and Celtics could be overcome by merely calling a timeout and giving the ball to one or the other of the 2 most pivotal players in the league. Let the defense come out double- and triple-teaming—Magic and Bird would find a way to get the ball to the open man. In many cases, Bird *was* the open man.

It looked like they might be playing with a sixth sense, something like court awareness. Was it nothing more than moving without the ball? Bird was so good at doing it, and magic was even more adept at taking advantage of it.

It seemed there was no stopping Magic or Bird, the Lakers or Celtics. The best any opponent could hope for was slowing them down with whatever means available. Yet on November 18, the Atlanta Hawks managed to take the ball right out of Magic's hands in the fourth quarter. All 7'4" of center Tom Burleson came crashing down on Earvin's left knee during a scrap for a loose ball in the fourth quarter.

The fun had ended; this was serious. Magic went under the arthroscope and the prognosis was not good. Torn cartilage and the ensuing surgery to clean it up would leave Earvin with a nasty 6" scar and out for at least 2 months. He figured it would be more like 3. The Lakers were 15–5 when he went down. A week later, a 120–114 loss to San Diego in the Forum marked the first time in 58 games that the Lakers had lost 2 in a row at home. They had only lost 4 in the Forum the entire previous season.

"It was the hardest thing I've ever had to deal with," said Earvin of his injury. "It's the most down I've ever been. It brings you down—pow—and things that were going oh-so-good are suddenly oh-so-bad."

Even Bird, however, couldn't stop Bird. A sciatic nerve problem at the base of his spine had been bothering Larry since the beginning of the season, yet in the first 7 games of 1980–81 he led the Celtics in scoring with an 18.4 average. It was tough to tell if Bird was injured—he kept mum. "Well, I thought it would go away, so I didn't tell anybody," he reasoned.

Nobody noticed any difference as Bird warmed up just in time for winter. On December 20 he faced Cleveland with 21 points and 20 rebounds, which was just a warmup for a Christmas Day clash with Philadelphia and the good Dr. J. The NBA on CBS and a national television audience was there to watch, and the best of Bird made for truly entertaining family viewing on the holiday. He pulled down 20 rebounds and scored 20 of his 28 points in the second half of a 117–108 victory for the Celtics. He was the most pivotal player of the game, with 4 straight hoops in a crucial fourth-quarter run. The last was a fadeaway base line jumper that put Boston ahead for good, 103–102. Bird played with so much explosive energy that he seemed more like a get-up-and-go-to guy.

"What you saw is what we see in Boston every night," said Coach Fitch. "Larry Bird was Larry Bird."

Alas, as 1980 gave way to 1981, Larry Bird fans saw something they had never seen before. In a game against the Golden State Warriors on January 2, 1981, Larry Bird did not score a point. The last time Larry Bird had been held scoreless was when the hoop was a coffee can and he'd been playing against his older brother Mark. Golden State registered a 121–106 upset as Bird went 0-for-9 from the field. It was the team's first loss in 14 games. Larry Bird was not Larry Bird.

Yet in the next three games—all wins—Bird poured in his usual 20-plus points per game and boxed out for all the big rebounds. But aside from a spinning drive to the bucket for a buzzer-beating, game-tying lay-up in a 117–111 overtime victory at Chicago, the rest was standard fare for Larry. He hit a 22-foot jumper to seal the Celtics seventeenth victory in their last 18 games—a 93–89 defeat of Philadelphia—but he seemed to be losing some of his energy.

Actually for Bird, this situation was a no-go. A hip injury put him on the bench in a 108–85 loss to Chicago on January 29, which broke Boston's 13-game winning streak. He dragged a charley horse through the next 3 games—all losses—and averaged only 12 points per outing in the process.

Only with their absences did Magic and Larry prove how valuable they were to the league. CBS set its sights on a March 1 doubleheader featuring Boston at Philly followed by Seattle at Los Angeles to test-market the appeal of the NBA. The exclusive contract CBS held with the NBA was up for renewel, so this was a do-or-die situation; CBS wanted more than anything to give the ball to Bird and Johnson. Magic did what he could to help the cause by filling in with some color commentary on the telecast, but he didn't exactly have an all-star performance on the air.

Finally, the moment the league had been waiting for came on February 27—a magic moment, so to speak. As the March 9, 1981 cover of *Sports Illustrated* proclaimed: "The Magic is Back." It had been 100 days since he last played, and to Earvin it seemed interminable. Still, was the Magic, the same old guy averaging 21.4 points per game and leading the NBA in assists and steals when he went down, really back? The last time anyone had seen him in public, Magic was grimacing instead of smiling. Could he resume his happy-go-lucky style of play?

"I can't play differently," said the Magic Man. "I got to play up to my own standards. Just hard, reckless abandon. You know, this thing was killing me. First, they take your ball away. That's bad. And then, not being around the guys on the team, that really hurt. That's my life, being around the fellas, talking jive, singing on the bus. All of the sudden, that's all taken away. I don't think missing the ball was all that important. Missing the fellas was badder than missing the ball."

Without Magic, the Lakers were 28–17. For the February 27 game against New Jersey, more than 17,000 buttons bearing "The Magic is Back" slogan were distributed. The media chronicled his every step. With 5:02 left in the first period, Magic checked into the game and the Lakers went to him immediately.

He had his ball back, and promptly threw right to the Nets' Maurice Lucas. He threw the next pass out of bounds. But Magic regained enough of his form to help lead the Lakers back from a 12-point deficit and whip the Nets, 107–103. He had 12 points and 11 rebounds, the last of which came on the offensive boards with the Lakers leading 105–103 with 10 seconds remaining. He even went diving for loose balls.

But Magic simply was not Magic. In that win over

the Nets he hit just 4 of 12 from the field, and he went 4 of 11 the next night in a loss to Phoenix. There were moments of greatness: As the season hit the stretch run, Earvin had 21 points, 16 rebounds, 10 assists, and 4 steals in a 118–104 win over San Antonio. The Magic was back as the Lakers hit 11 of 12 shots to start the second quarter. Johnson was off and running, and closed out the regular season with 27 points, 9 rebounds, 7 assists, and 5 steals in a 122–116 win over San Diego. The Lakers came down this stretch just a neck behind Phoenix, however, and their 54–28 regular-season record left them in second place in the Atlantic and with a best-of-three miniseries against Houston to start the 1981 playoffs.

Magic's net worth to the team was as readily seen in the attendance figures as anything else. When he was out of the lineup, attendance dropped by an average of 1,141 fans per game. Multiply that by 45 games, then by $20 or so per ticket to figure the lost revenue.

But money was no object; the team concept had been interrupted. Magic had been the ultimate team player, but because his return attracted so much attention, he was singled out. After his first game back, the locker room had been emptied for more than an hour—except for Earvin, who was still answering questions and had not yet taken a shower.

"I guess he was human," said Lakers' coach Westhead, "but it's only a guess. When Magic wasn't with us our performance was surgical, neat, clean, minimal talking, no nonsense. But when Magic returned it was like Looney Tunes. He created havoc. Everybody started laughing again. It was unreal."

Magic seemed to get off to a good start in the first

game of the playoffs. He had 26 in the opener against Houston, but the Rockets won at the Forum 111–107. A tough loss.

Magic stayed up until 5 A.M. the morning following the first loss. This had to be a nightmare. He fouled out of game 2, even though the Lakers managed to escape Houston with a 111–106 win to force a third and final game. In that final game, the Lakers trailed 87–86 with 30 seconds left when Westhead was forced to call the final play. Clearly, the choice had to be to go to the big guy. But the coach went to his go-to guy. Magic drove the lane to try and make the pivotal play. He forced up a shot that hit nothing but . . . nothing. An airball ended a 2-for-14 shooting night (10 points) and the 1981 season for the Lakers.

Magic didn't know what to say; he made no excuses. "It was just one of those things. I could say I got hit on the drive. I did get hit on the elbow when I shot, but I held back and didn't follow through."

Outside the West Coast, this whole ordeal was not news. Bird was stealing all the headlines by leading the Celtics to a 62–20 record and another Atlantic Division championship. The regular season for the Celtics had come down to one game, the final game against Philadelphia. The winner went home with the division title and a week's vacation courtesy of a rest through the first round of the playoffs. The loser would be relegated to a miniseries. Bird scored 20 of his 24 points in the second half of the 108–101 win and thereby proved that as a go-to guy nobody did it better.

Bird was serving notice that the Celtics could go to him as much as necessary in the playoffs. Boston drew Chicago in the semifinals of the Eastern Conference playoffs, and it was Larry who scored 35 points on 13-for-22 shooting and grabbed 11 rebounds as Boston beat Chicago 109–103 on April 12 to finish off a 4-game sweep in the best-of-7 series.

But would Bird and the Celtics have enough go-go juice left to make a run at the NBA championship? When the Celtics went down 3 games to 1 to the Sixers in the Eastern finals, it seemed as though Boston was running on empty. The series went the full 7 games, and 5 of those were decided by 2 points or less. The first game of the series featured 27 lead changes. In the only blowout, a 118–99 victory for Boston in game 2, Bird had 34 points on 14-for-21 shooting and 16 rebounds. In the fourth-quarter run that put the game away, Bird didn't key the Celtics offense. He *was* the Celtics offense.

"Football has its student body left and right, and we were running our Larry Bird left and Larry Bird right," Fitch said afterward. "If he's hitting like he was tonight, the I want to make sure he's getting the ball every time down."

Yet the Celtics fell behind 3–1 in games in the series, and they had to go to Bird to bail out the team. He started out the fifth game shooting 2-for-8 but came back with 32 points, 11 rebounds, and 5 assists in a 111–109 Boston win. In the sixth game, Larry had 25 points, 16 rebounds, and a 22-foot turnaround jumper that put the Celtics ahead for good with 1:04 to play in the 100–98 victory. Larry had said that if the Celtics won game 6 the Sixers would be "in trouble." So with 1:03 to play in the series finale, Bird prepared to make good on his word. He calmly spotted up, arced the ball back over his head from 15 feet—can you picture it?

—and banked in the shot that put the Celtics ahead 91–89. The final score was 91–90.

"I wanted the ball in my hands for that last shot," Bird said. "Not in anybody else's hands in the world. I knew we would win it."

Could the Celtics just give Bird the ball and run away with the NBA title? Houston had emerged from the Western Conference as the other contender for the championship, and the Rockets had finished the regular season with a 40–42 record—22 less victories than Boston. The Celtics figured to run Houston right out of the gym. Boston's 98–95 victory in game one seemed to be routine. Bird even came down on one offensive series and missed a jumper from the foul line. But sometimes even Bird's misses are spectacular.

On this one, he followed his shot to the right side of the basket, grabbed the long rebound with his right hand, moved the ball back left, and canned the shot jumper without ever touching the ground. The move was mimicked on playgrounds and in YMCAs throughout American for the next several weeks, and as the years went by, when people talked about Bird they were still talking about this play. "One of the greatest plays of all time," cried Celtics general manager Red Auerbach. "I've never seen anything like it. Just magnificent."

Houston hung in, and it took a 109–80 rout in game 5 for the Celtics to take a 3–2 lead. As game 6 was set to start, M.L. Carr walked up to Bird and said, "You've got to carry us tonight. Added Bird: "Every time I went to the bench, the guys said, 'You've got to win this for us.' " Bird scored 7 of his 27 points in the final 4 minutes as the Celtics held a slim lead.

The pivotal play in the game naturally came with

time running down. Boston had blown an 84–67 lead, and now Houston trailed by just 3 points. Clearly, there was no other way to go. Bird hit a 15-footer to thwart one comeback, then threw a perfect lob pass to Maxwell for a lay-up. Then with time running out, he backed in the defense, turned to his right, and launched a 3-point swish.

"Larry Bird is such a money player," said the Celtics' Chris Ford as he raised his champagne glass and toast to Bird and the 1981 NBA championship. "And when the money was on the line, he came through. We needed life and Larry was there."

Two years into their professional careers and Magic had won one NBA championship and Larry had won the other. That was enough to make them the big men in the league, if not the big guys. Whether the game was in the final 30 seconds or the final 30 minutes, the ball had to go to Bird or Magic. If nothing else, they made the game's final fling fun, and as the Magic Man had often said, fun is what the game is all about.

All of which brings us to another most intriguing question. What do a couple of fun-loving guys like Earvin and Larry do to amuse themselves during the off-season? If the summer of 1981 was any indication, Johnson and Bird went back home to play ball. As soon as Larry returned to Springs Valley and right after Magic sat down and had 2 or 3 helpings of his mother's sweet potatoes, they went out to throw around that little old ball—softball. Magic Johnson was the tallest third baseman in the league for his favorite team, "The Magic Johnsons," and Bird can played for his club, "The West Baden Police."

Mornings consisted of working out with weights and shooting around for a couple of hours. Bird even had a regulation court built in his backyard to get in his practice. But all work and no play would leave Larry or Magic with a dull smile, so they each started their own basketball camps. Magic had one in L.A. and one in Lansing; Bird did one in Boston and one in French Lick. No camper left without a full complement of clothing and equipment. What made the games really fun was when Larry or Magic would play one-on-five with a group of 8-year-olds until the sun went down. A friend suggested to Bird that he should let the media come in and see how he played with the kids.

"Never," claimed Bird. And so it was.

Both Bird and Magic came back for the 1981–82 season ready to take the game into their hands. Bird had finished the previous season with an average of 21.2 points per game as well as 10 rebounds and 5 assists. Magic averaged 21.6 points, 9 assists, and 8 rebounds, numbers men with 5 times their experience couldn't approach. Bird was sixteenth in the league in scoring and fourth in rebounding. Magic led the league in steals with 3.43 per game; he would have won the assists title had he played in enough games to qualify. And the really amazing thing was that they were both still improving.

Some integral off-season happenings set the stage for the show the 1981–82 season was about to become. Bird finished second to Julius Earving in the balloting for the Player of the Year in NBA. He had also been the second choice to Cedric Maxwell in the voting for the MVP of the playoffs. If there was one thing Bird worked for hours on end *not* to be, it was second best. He needed no other incentive to try harder. In June, Magic signed a 25-year, $25 million contract, the first long-term, big-time contract in the history of the NBA. Some suspected that Magic's future beyond playing was in management. Some suspected he already *was* management. An anonymous owner of another team even jibed, ''In twenty years there will be three basketball teams in the NBA. I'll own one, and Magic Johnson will own the other two.'' The bottom line meant that he was now most definitely the Lakers' money man.

Magic was right on the money once he got the ball back. In his first 3 pre-season games, he averaged 20 points, 14.3 assists, and 13 rebounds per game. He *averaged* a triple double. He finished the 8 pre-season games with averages of 10 assists, 9 rebounds, and 2 assists per game, all of which led the team. He was second in scoring at 18 per game.

Once again, more than 13,000 season tickets were sold for Celtics' home games. The regular season opener was the thirty-first straight sellout in the Garden. Needless to say, Celtics' owner Harry Mangurian had the return on his investment. Even Bird knew he had given the Celtics more than their money's worth, and he said so. ''I think Mr. Mangurian made a good move when he signed me,'' Larry said.

Bird could laugh. The Celtics were off to a 9–1 start and a good time was being had by all involved. Bird's smiling face was used in 7-Up, Spalding, and Converse commercials. He was also the poster person in advertisements for the Sun Life of Canada Insurance Company. Magic's mug was plastered on every billboard in Los Angeles. His commercial for 7-Up was critically acclaimed, and he did a great spot for Buick with jockey Willie Shoemaker.

When they weren't shooting in-your-face fadeaway jumpers, Magic and Bird were leading the league in face time. CBS thought so as well after the 1980–81 season returned the biggest Neilson ratings for the pro game in several years. The NBA on CBS also received a new long-term contract. And if the nation's living rooms and bar rooms were concerned, Magic and Bird were quickly becoming basketball's most familiar faces.

It doesn't take much to make Earvin or Larry happy. Give them each the ball, let them run the break, and realize that is doesn't get any better than this. People in and around Los Angeles called this free-wheelin' and dealin' style "Showtime," and Boston fashioned its own version of life in the fast lane as a way to run, gun, and have fun.

But the Lakers were slow getting out of the gates at the start of the regular season. They lost the opener to Houston on national television in double overtime. L.A. staggered to a 2–4 start, and all was not well with Magic. Through the first 11 games of the season he had averaged 17.4 points and a league-leading 10 assists. But he said he wasn't having fun anymore. Westhead decided that the ball needed to go to the big guy more, and so he designed a new offense for the 1981 season which was intended to get the ball to Kareem. The team rebounded to go to 9–4, and perhaps the Lakers were about to hit stride with their fifth straight win, a 113–110 triumph at Utah on November 22.

After the game, however, Westhead called Johnson into his office to discuss what he termed "a lack of concentration." That could have meant Magic hadn't listened or decided that he knew best when the game was on the line, or that he didn't give up the ball when he was supposed to. Later that night, Johnson was ready to pull the plug. He said he couldn't play under Westhead's system and that he wanted to be traded.

The full-court press was on. Magic alerted the media to his feelings, and the next morning the Lakers' owner, Jerry Buss, called a press conference. Westhead was unemployed moments later, with the remaining 3 years of his 4-year contract guaranteed.

But this situation was about more than money. Assistant coach Pat Riley was designated to take charge with general manager Jerry West lending a hand. Some anticipated that the ballgame had been turned over to Magic. Johnson was Buss's good friend; they were often seen together on the L.A. social circuit. Word was that perhaps Magic had prompted Buss to give Westhead the word *go*—as in get out of town.

Magic declined comment; Buss talked. "There was a lack of excitement on offense that I wanted to see," Buss reasoned. "I enjoyed Showtime and I want to see it again. I'm speaking as much as a fan as anything else."

The fans greeted Magic with boos before Riley's first game as head coach. But against San Antonio that night, November 24, Magic turned the jeers to cheers with 20 points, 16 assists, 10 rebounds, 3 steals, and a blocked shot in a 136–116 trashing of the Spurs. In Westhead's last 5 games, the Lakers had won by a total of 11 points, and now they had almost doubled that sum. That in itself doubled Magic's pleasure and his fun.

"Yeah, I'm happy and so are him and him." said Johnson, pointing to his teammates, Norm Nixon, Jammal Wilkes, and even Kareem, who was so enthused he even was out filling the lanes on the fast break of newly revived running game Los Angeles showcased in the San Antonio victory. "This is the way it was two years ago when we were getting those easy buckets," said Earvin, excitedly. "You see the way we were moving tonight? Pow-pow-pow. See the way Kareem was handling the ball out there? When he gets into that mood, watch out!"

With Westhead running the team in slow motion, the Lakers averaged 108 points per game. Riley flipped the switch and bright-lights basketball returned to the West Coast. In the first 4 games under their new coach, Los Angeles averaged 128 points per game.

"Do we look like a different team? Now there is more movement in the offense. When there's a chance for everybody to get involved, it's a lot easier for everybody to be happy." That's what Norm Nixon, Magic's backcourt running mate, finally said about the whole ordeal a month after it happened. By then Magic had been running so much the incident was nothing more than a blur in the rear-view mirror. Showtime was back, and the show was only beginning.

Larry was intent on playing any role his team had in mind. As Steve Hershey wrote in *The Sporting News*, "Bird, of course, is the one player who can do anything any basketball coach can dream up." On December 25, he was able to show off his crowd-pleasing defense. Philadelphia was in town and leading the Sixers was the sharp shooting guard Andrew Toney, who was the one player the Celtics had not been able to stop in the previous season. Toney scored 22 points, including 7 in a row in the fourth quarter, when Bird was thrust into the role of shutting down the gunslinger. High noon and a showdown at the Garden. An Oscar-winning performance with rave reviews as Bird held Toney to 2 points the rest of the way in Boston's 111–103 victory.

Perhaps it is an innate quality in all stars that they some day want to direct the big picture. Bird went on an 8-game tear during January of 1982 when he averaged 26 points, 13 rebounds, and 5.5. assists per outing. He started that flurry with 40 points 16 rebounds, and 7 assists in a game that enabled him to leave the Garden to a standing ovation on January 10. Bird had established himself as a 4-star performer in the NBA, and it was just a matter of acting naturally for him. Yes, he was going to be a star; watch him drive and dish off to M.L. Carr.

What would he do for an encore? How about 18-for-24 shooting and 38 points in a 111–107 win over the New York Knicks on January 19? At that point of the season, Bird was eighth in the league in scoring with 22.6 average, fourth in rebounds at 10 per game, and he was leading the NBA forwards in assists with 5, which was also better than half the guards in the league.

Accordingly, the Celtics and the Lakers were planning on an extended run. What could close down this act now? On January 28, Larry Bird, who had built his reputation on being in the right place at the right time, was caught in the wrong place. All that time moving without the ball, and when Bird was standing still in the third quarter of a game against Milwaukee, Harvey Catchings drilled his elbow into Larry's cheekbone. It was shattered on the spot. But the show must go on: Bird finished the game and scored 11 points in the fourth quarter of a 106–102 victory. He didn't miss a beat, though he did leave the starting lineup for the next

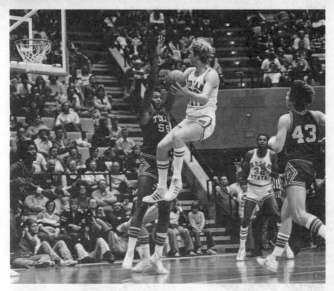

Bird drives the lane against Tulsa and goes into the air, all the while looking for an open teammate on the base line. (©Indiana State University Sports Information Department)

Larry and Dominique Wilkins of the Atlanta Hawks played out their personal one-on-one in the Eastern Conference semifinal series of the 1988 playoffs. In game four Bird attempted to cut off a Wilkins drive to the bucket. In game seven, Bird scored 20 points in the fourth quarter to help the Celtics win the series. (©Wide World Photos)

Bird has always been effective at stepping into the passing lane to make great defensive plays. Such was the way he was able to steal this inbounds pass intended for Utah's Ben Poquette. (©AP/Wide World Photos)

Red Auerbach was able to light up many a victory cigar once Larry Bird became a Celtic. Auerbach, president and general manager of the Celtics, drafted Bird as a junior eligible out of Indiana State, and two years later he called him the ''greatest forward to ever play the game.'' (©AP/ Wide World Photos)

Bird was the toast of the town after he helped Boston win the 1981 NBA championship. Similar parades greeted him and his teammates after they won NBA titles for Boston in 1984 and 1986. (©AP/Wide World Photos)

Larry Bird's kind of town was Terre Haute. After winning the NBA's Most Valuable Player award in 1984, Mayor Pete Chalos gave Bird the key to the city. There is also a street named after Bird in Terre Haute. (©AP/Wide World Photos)

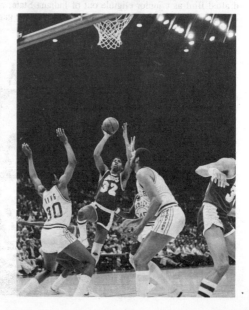

When there was one second left in the game and the Lakers needed only one basket to win, they went to Magic Johnson to take the final shot. He hit this one over Golden State's Joe Barry Caroll to beat the Warriors 120–118 in 1981. (©AP/Wide World Photos)

When Magic Johnson was hanging with one-time teammate Norm Nixon he was always smiling. Here, they had some good times while practicing for the 1985 NBA All-Star Game. (©AP/Wide World Photos)

After being made the number one selection in the 1979 NBA college draft, Earvin Johnson is presented to the media by Lakers' general manager Jerry West. (©AP/Wide World Photos)

Lights, camera, and action take place outside Magic's Bel Air mansion where he was filming a music video with Larry Bird. "Choose Your Weapon" premiered in February of 1986 with the Loverboy hit single, "Working for the Weekend," as the soundtrack. (©AP/Wide World Photos)

Michael Jordan needed to put a hand on Earvin just to stop him in the 1987 NBA All-Star Game. (©AP/Wide World Photos)

Earvin battled Bird on the boards during their first meeting as professionals on December 28, 1979, in the Forum in Los Angeles. (©AP/Wide World Photos)

That smile could only mean that Magic Johnson was just named the Most Valuable Player in the NBA after the 1987 season. (©AP/Wide World Photos)

5 games. He reappeared as a starter in the All-Star Game and earned Most Valuable Player honors in that contest. With Bird in the role of an understudy, the team won 5 straight, including a rousing victory over Philadelphia in which Larry came off the bench to score 29 points.

It was becoming quite difficult to find something new and different to write about Magic or the Bird at this point. Magic scored 40 points in a return visit to Michigan when the Lakers beat the Pistons. And when Detroit came to L.A. 2 weeks later, Earvin had the fans dancing in the aisles with a triple double. When the Celtics lost back-to-back home games to Seattle and Portland at the end of January, headlines in the Boston *Globe* pointed out that it was the first time the club had lost back-to-back home games since Bird came to town. Likewise, when Boston put together a franchise-record 18-game winning streak late in the season, it was front-page news. The last time the Celtics had made such a clamor was in 1959–60, when the team won 17 in a row.

Conjuring up past accomplishments was becoming a ritual, for Larry and Magic were only beginning to rewrite the record books in the NBA. As the season came down the stretch, Earvin became the first player since 1972 to record 600 assists and 600 rebounds in the same season. By season's end he would be the first to dish out 700 assists and pull down 700 rebounds in one year since Wilt Chamberlain had done it in 1968. As Boston finished the regular season in first place in the Atlantic Division with a 63–19 record and as Los Angeles won the Pacific Division with a 57–25 mark, it seemed to set the stage for perhaps the greatest playoff series in the history of the NBA.

It would be a week after the end of the regular season before either the Celtics or the Lakers would spring into playoff action. But Magic smiled and played this waiting game with all the vehemence of any competition. He was getting ready to put on a show to remember. The only thing the Phoenix Suns were able to remember after the Lakers had swept 4 straight to win the Western Conference semifinals was that Magic had a triple double in each of the victories, only the last of which—a 122–107 count—was by less than 12 points.

Looking back on the 1982 playoffs, Bird seemed overshadowed. He wasn't playing his best basketball. His 26 points in a 131–126 defeat of Washington to clinch the Eastern Conference semifinal series was the first performance worth noting. The Celtics went on to battle Philly in an Eastern final reminiscent of the 1981 series. Boston went down 3 games to 1, came back to tie at 3-3, but the seventh game went to the Sixers. As the curtain came down on the Celtics, Bird was off in the wings wondering about his 7-for-18 shooting and scoreless fourth quarter in the final game.

That the Lakers went on to win the 1982 NBA championship by blowing out the rest of the league was no surprise. Magic tried to play a supporting role as the Lakers swept 4 games straight from Phoenix and San Antonio before finally suffering its first playoff loss, 110–94, to Philly in the second game of the finals. But as L.A. took that series 4 games to 2, Magic went out of his way to set up Bob McAdoo, Nixon, and Kareem in starring roles. Like Bird, Earvin wanted everyone to realize how good the entire cast was. Johnson averaged a triple double throughout the playoffs and finished the final game of the championship series with 13 points, 13 rebounds, and 13 assists.

Still, as he was awarded the trophy for Most Valuable Player in the playoffs for the second time in his career, Magic decided to direct the attention elsewhere. The only reason he was able to get off and running is because there were teammates running right alongside.

"To me, it's the greatest high in basketball. There you are, in the middle, getting ready to create something. It's like dancing to music. It's like Freddy Astaire. And this team, this is a boogie-woogie team. We all have our own styles, but as a team we dance real well."

There was the NBA, all alone and dancing in the dark. Then the spotlights turned to Magic and the Bird and it was Showtime.

The common denominator between the Celtics' run to the 1981 title and the Lakers spring to the 1982 championship is that come next season they were still talking about what had happened the previous spring. Whereas prior to the 1981–82 season, the Celtics were being called Larry's team, similar accolades were being directed toward Earvin as the 1982–83 campaign was set to tip off. All the great gurus of the game were able to voice their opinions when the national magazines previewed the upcoming season, and as Milwaukee coach Don Nelson was assessing the Lakers for the upcoming year, he said, "They have Magic, who can play anywhere he wants. With his sacrifices, Magic was the man who made that team last year. Without him, they definitely don't win the championship."

But to put these formidable years of the 1980s in proper perspective it is best to look back on the 1982–83 season as a whole. The pattern was being set: Either Magic's team or Larry's team would win the NBA title.

Consider what the Philadelphia 76ers went through to break that run. With Julius Erving, Darryl Dawkins, Bobby Jones, Maurice Cheeks, Andrew Toney, Doug Collins, and Steve Mix, among others, the Sixers had the makings of the most dominant team of the eighties. But the Sixers were missing something. With no Bird or Johnson or anything close available, Philadelphia went out and signed Moses Malone, the league's best big guy, to a contract. And even with Moses, Philly had to go 65–17 to finish 9 games ahead of the Celtics and break their 3-year stronghold on the Atlantic Division title. And even with Moses, the Sixers still had to battle through 4 rousing games to defeat the Lakers in the NBA finals. And it wasn't until the Sixers had beaten out both the Lakers and Celtics that they could be compared to Boston and L.A. and the other greatest teams of all time.

Consequently, the 1982–83 season was somewhat uneventful only because Magic and the Bird did not put forth a championship effort. But it was only measured as such because their Herculean tasks of the previous years were looked on as mere mortal accomplishments. To be gods they had to play more god-like basketball. Finally, on March 30, 1983, Bird scored 53 points— the most in his professional career to date and the second-best point total up to 1988—in a 142–116 win over Indiana. He did all that in just 33 minutes. And so what if Magic led the league in assists with a 9.9 average? Finally, on January 13, he had a career high-to-date 21 assists in a 122–101 win at Atlanta. That was more like it.

What do Magic and Larry remember about the 1982–83 season? The Celtics were the league's peskiest team.

They stopped a New Jersey winning streak at 12 games and a Laker run at 7 straight. The Knicks came into the Garden on a 5-game string and fell flat. The defending champion Sixers came in riding the crest of a 10-game winning wave, but the Celtics came up with the ultimate dunk of Philly. (Make a note of this: In busting New Jersey, Bird led the game with 33 points, 12 rebounds, 6 assists, and 2 steals. He said afterwards, "I lost my concentration.") As for Earvin, well, that was the season Kareem's mansion in Bel Air burned down. The big guy lost his entire 3,000-album collection. To E.J. the Deejay—another of Magic's many handles—that was the greatest loss of the season.

The most stunning loss of the season came in the second round of the Eastern Conference playoffs. That the Celtics had to play a miniseries against Atlanta was a sign of troubled times. That it took 3 games to dispose of the Hawks was the result of the continuous injury problems and lineup changes the team endured.

"The bottom line is that we're still the Celtics," Bird said. "Ask L.A. and Philadelphia who they fear, and I'll bet they say us."

The Celtics never made it that far. In the Eastern Conference semifinals, Milwaukee swept Boston with 4 straight victories. The bottom line on Bird was 23.6 points per game to finish eleventh in the league in scoring. He was tenth in rebounding with an 11.0 average, one more than the previous year when he finished fourth in the NBA. He was ninth in the league in foul shooting by hitting 84%, and he led the Celtics in every category including steals and assists. But that wasn't the way he looked at it.

"We never really got a string going," said the ultimate teammate. "It seemed like we'd win four, lose two, win four, lose two. There were so many changes in the lineup that there were times when we didn't move the ball around like in the past; the flow and the timing were a step behind."

Perhaps the Lakers were just a step slower than the previous season as well. Yet L.A. blew by Portland, 4 games to 1, in the Western Conference semifinals. San Antonio was a bit more of a problem, but Los Angeles prevailed in 6 games. Still, the Lakers weren't winning games so much by running and gunning. Down the stretch, Magic shared the ball with Nixon and Wilkes and Cooper and said, "We have so many guys on this team who can lead the break. Isn't it beautiful?" Magic led the league in assists with a 10.5 average and added 8.7 rebounds and 16.8 points. He was eighth in the league in steals.

But when the full-court press was on in the end, Earvin was conspicuous by his absence. In 3 of the past 4 years, Magic ended the season by telling everyone to get up and dance. The only time Magic *wasn't* boogying in the end, the nation's fans raised their glasses and toasted Bird and the Celtics. It wasn't supposed to end this way. But Magic and the Bird could still smile, as if to say, "It isn't over until we decide it is." In other words, the show must go on.

INSTANT REPLAY
The Star of Stars

THE BRENDAN BYRNE MEADOWLANDS ARENA WAS BUZZ-
ing. From press row to the last row to the front row,
more than 20,000 fans were having an open conversation about what was transpiring in the 1982 NBA All-
Star Game. This was the moment when everyone started
talking about Larry Bird.

With 6:48 remaining in the game, the Bird Man rose
up off the Eastern Conference All-Stars' bench and showed
why he was becoming the talk of the league. At the
time, the East was trailing the West 105–103. Bird
turned on the first sellout crowd in Byrne Arena history
by scoring 12 of his team's final 15 points in leading
the East to a 120–118 victory. The press couldn't say
enough about Bird, naming him the Most Valuable
Player. The compliments extended all the way to the
locker room. In Boston they still talk about this outing
of January 31, 1982, as more than just another game.

Back in the Eastern Conference dressing room the players had nothing but great things to say. Artis Gilmore, Bob Lanier, Michael Ray Richardson, and even the good Dr. J himself were all having the last word on the subject of Larry Bird.

"I'll tell you," said Gilmore, the 7' 2" center of the Chicago Bulls, "it was good for a change to sit on the bench and watch Bird perform well for your team instead of doing us in. That's the nice thing about playing on the same team with Larry Bird. Whatever he's doing out there, he's not doing it to me."

Celtics coach Bill Fitch seemed almost prophetic with his comments about the All-Star Game exactly the year before. When Bird was not among the top 5 vote getters among the Eastern Conference forwards in the 1981 NBA All-Star balloting, Fitch fumed. "I haven't seen five forwards better than him in my eleven years. This just isn't indicative of the situation. He's the one putting the people in the arenas."

The 20,149 fans who were there that Sunday afternoon in 1982 still talk about Bird's exploits. In the first half, Larry left the fans with a flurry that was a sign of what was to come. With 8:14 left in the second quarter, Bird checked into the game with the East leading 45–38. The East then reeled off a 20–4 run, and Bird didn't score a point. He merely ran this Showtime with 4 rebounds and 4 assists.

With 6:48 left in the game and the East leading by a bucket after holding a 105–97 lead with 8 minutes left, Fitch didn't hesitate to point his finger of blame. He motioned Bird off the bench, and this was the moment everyone, Bird included, had been waiting for. "I wanted to get back in for the last six minutes," Larry said. "I was ready to take the challenge. When the game goes down to the wire, my team looks for me to shoot or to pass.''

With Celtic teammates Robert Paris and Tiny Archibald on the floor, Bird was the guy all the players wanted to go to. Boom! Bird hit a fadeaway from the top of the key for a score of 107–103, which quickly disappeared. Bird struck from the foul line for 2 free throws to tie the game at 109 with 5:03 remaining. In the next minute, twice Bird backed in on the defense and turned to swish a 20-foot J. The Doc set him up for a final jumper at 2:37 which put the East up 118–114, and then Bird hit 2 free throws to spell the final margin of victory.

"When it got down to money time, they just called my plays,'' Bird said. "My teammates like to go to me in the clutch. If I hit my first shot, I keep shooting. If I start missing, I got to the pass. Earlier in the game, I was struggling some, but when I got back I was ready for the challenge.''

When Bird came back into the game with 6:48 remaining, MVP balloting had just become the topic of conversation among the media. One even considered a write-in vote for the San Diego Chicken, who up until then had put on what may have been the best performance of the afternoon. But when all was totaled, Bird had 86 votes and Celtic teammate Parish was second with 39. To Bird it was just another game, and everyone else was beginning to think so, too.

"I don't care if it's a pickup game, a practice, or a championship game,'' said Los Angeles coach Pat Riley, who also coached the Western All-Stars. "Bird plays the same. He really hurts us with those closing-second jumpers. It was Bird's effort down the stretch which made the difference.''

The Doc may have put it best. ''No matter what has to be done,'' Erving said, ''Larry can do it. And he likes the pressure. Another thing, he makes the other players on his team better and that makes for a winning team.''

Then again, Bob Lanier, the 6′ 11″ center of the Milwaukee Bucks, had plenty to say. ''What a marvelous player. I can't say enough about him. He has the team concept—that's why he's a winner. He'd be a winner on the playground, he'd be a winner anywhere. He doesn't have to score to be a winner. He knows that a pat on the back is as important as a basket. Larry Bird is my man.''

Michael Ray Richardson, then of the New York Knicks, had this to say: ''He's a great ballplayer. He's always playing team ball, no matter what. He always does what he has to do, especially when the game is on the line.''

It seems they could never say enough about Larry Bird.

6

Winning Ways

LARRY BIRD WAS PUTTING ON A SHOW BY WAY OF BURY-
ing a bevy of downtown jump shots. He came off a
Robert Parish screen and hit the stand-up, baseline J,
then he ran circles around his defender in order to free
himself for a swish from the top of the key. He brought
the Celtics back to within one point, and Boston had the
ball for one final shot. Coach K.C. Jones called timeout
and designed a play to go to Cedric Maxwell for the last
shot. Bird took it upon himself to let the final flurry fly
anyway. He made it. He knew he had it all along. Nice
play, K.C.

Magic Johnson was making this performance look
like a game of bumper pool. He slashed through the
lane and made the Phoenix Suns feel as if they were
standing still. Follow the bouncing ball; there it goes on
a funny angle seemingly off James Worthy's hand and
through the hoop in one perpetual motion.

The shots hadn't been falling for Larry Bird as the 1985 NBA playoffs began. Not a slump, he insisted; "I just was missing shots I should have made." So the Bird went out 3 hours before the next game and took more than 300 shots in practice. He made well over 300 if you count the multitude that he swished in the game that night. This was just one of those night when Larry was a can't-miss kid.

"Our half coming up, our half," boasted Magic Johnson as he was recovering from a dislocated finger so bad it looked like it belonged on his foot. The Lakers had been in a slump while Earvin missed 13 games of the 1983–84 season, but that couldn't keep him from his appointed playoff rounds. This was only December and Magic was already talking title.

Larry Bird was covered with champagne and Magic Johnson was covered with soap. Such a contrast between winner and losers: after taking the 1984 championship, Bird found his cheers at the bottom of the bottle while Magic drowned his tears in the shower.

What would be the twilight of any normal player's career became the highlight of Magic and Larry's lives. Moments only Earvin and Larry could relate to began happening with increasing frequency, for how they played the game now mattered as much as winning and losing. Winning may not have been everything, but by the time they rolled midway into the era of the 1980s and into what was the midpoint—and the high point—of their pro careers, Magic and Larry both had that feeling: If they played their games as only they could, then winning would no longer be everything; it would be the *only* thing.

Johnson and Bird were part of an exclusive winners'

circle. They were quickly developing a ways to their
means, and the end result was obvious. "Lets face it,"
said Lakers' coach Pat Riley. "When Magic and Bird
take the floor they know they're going to win. Every
one else is trying to win." And when they were taken
out of context and left to stand alone, Larry and Earvin
seemed to have a winning way about their persona. It
wasn't just the phenomenon of the Johnson smile anymore, and there certainly was no mystique to Bird being
"The Hick from French Lick." Yet they both exhibited
a way to go about winning that set them apart from
Kareem, Moses, and the Doctor—and most of the rest
of the best who ever played the game.

Every once in a decade or so, the professional game
is elevated to a sublime match-up. The NBA reached
one such peak in 1969, when 6′ 9″ center Bill Russell led
the Boston Celtics into the NBA championship series
against 7′1″ center Wilt Chamberlain and the Los Angeles Lakers. It was a classic playoff and a classic con-
frontation, one against which all other finals had been
measured. Russell and Wilt both put out the best of
their winning ways, but the Celtics prevailed 4 games to
3.

Yet in 1984 and 1985 the NBA enjoyed its 2
winningest moments, against which all championship
series past and present and all eras of basketball will
forever be measured, more so than the series in 1969.
The Celtics beat the Lakers in 7 games in 1984; L.A.
came back to take the finals in 6 the following season.
In the process, Magic and Bird went about their game
of one-on-one-upmanship with a whole new vim and
vigor.

Was this Wilt and Russell all over again, or was this

something better? As Magic and Bird prepared to do battle in the 1984 finals, people in the know were downplaying the encounter.

"It's like the opening of a great play. Everybody is waiting to see it," said the Lakers' general manager, Jerry West, who played in those games with Russell and Chamberlain. "If Bird and Magic played against each other, then it would be real special. As much as people want to talk about who's the best, you'd get a better idea who plays the greater total game if they matched up against each other."

Said Bill Fitch, who was coaching in Houston at the time, "It's like comparing a quarterback to a fullback. "You can say they're both backs, but their jobs and duties are completely different."

Could it have been that Magic and Bird were so incomparable that it was only sensible to compare them to each other?

"I don't think there's much difference between us at all," said Bird before the 1984 finals began. "He's out there to win and I am, too. As far as individual things, I think we're both basically pretty even. He handles the ball a little better, and I shoot a little better. That's about it. You can get down to all these details you want to get down to. But I compare Magic Johnson to me in the respect that he's a winner just like I am."

So how is it that Bird and Johnson deserve to have a realm of their own? Numbers tell part of the story, and much more than mere statistical prowess. Prior to the 1983–84 season, Bird joined Magic in the joy of long-term, big-money contracts. Originally it was reported that Bird signed a 7-year pact worth $15 million. At better than $2 million a year, that made him the highest-paid player in the game. It was, however, a $12 million deal over 7 years, but at $1.8 million a year Bird was still the highest paid player in the game. If the return on investment would be anything like what the Lakers reaped when they signed Magic to such a long contract, then this was another true value.

On the bottom line, however, was winning. And that was the top priority to Magic and Larry. Johnson started the season with 4 straight triple doubles. He had 29 points, 14 assists, and 12 rebounds in a 126–118 win at Detroit, which was hitting close to home as far as Earvin was concerned. Five nights later on November 13, Johnson scored 30 points with 16 assists and 11 rebounds in a 124–118 win over Utah for the forty-ninth triple double in a little more than 4 years of pro ball. On November 11, Bird buried a bevy of jumpers in the process of scoring a season-high 39 points in a 133–124 win over Detroit. This was all getting to be the status quo, and the bottom line one month into the season read that the Celtics were 8–1 and in first place in the Atlantic Division, while the Lakers were 6–2 and leading the Pacific Division.

The rest of the Lakers could have provided testimony to Magic's winning ways. On December 12, he was reaching for a loose ball and crunched his right index finger on either the rock or Derek Harper of the Dallas Mavericks. The finger was dislocated so badly he missed 13 games. The Lakers went 7–6 during that time. At the time he went out, he was averaging 15 assists a game. In the first game without Magic, L.A. passed off for a meager 14 assists as a team.

It wasn't hard to identify Bird as a winner. In the middle of January, 1984, he went on a shooting spree

that showed he was the best in the game. He struck for
35 points and 8 assists on January 9 as the Celtics won
their fourth straight. He had 36 the next night in a win
over Dallas, and 3 nights later scored 29 points, 19
rebounds, and 8 assists in a 105–104 win at Philadelphia. He went into a slump with 8 points on 3-for-13
shooting in the next game against Milwaukee. Check
that; he was just missing some shots he should have
made. In the next game he had 38 points, 13 assists,
and 9 rebounds in a 122–113 win at Kansas City.

That is what made Bird a winner. As Charlie Vincent
wrote in *The Sporting News*, ''The secret to Bird is
work ethic. Julius Erving is the precise surgeon, and
Earvin Johnson is the magician. Bird has been described as the carpenter. Bird the carpenter, banging
away, hammering and pounding until he gets the job
done.''

In the game of the greatest one-on-one players, Magic
seemed to do one better than every other player in the
1984 NBA All-Star Game in Denver. He wheeled and
hit good buddy Mark Aguirre or he would deal it inside
to Kareem in the process of handing out an All-Star
Game record of 22 assists. Magic even hit a hanging
jumper in the lane—you know the one where his hand
looks like a big baseball mitt and his arm looks like it is
stuck in suspended animation—at the final buzzer to
force an overtime. But the East beat the West, 154–145,
and Magic's other good buddy, Isiah Thomas, was
named the Most Valuable Player. Yet with Boston sporting the league's best record at 38–9 and the Lakers
leading the Western Conference with a 30–16 mark, it
was becoming apparent that all the other players would

be watching while Magic and Bird went one-on-one for final victory.

It seemed the last 3 months of the season were little more than a formality. Bird hit for 33 points with 13 rebounds and 13 assists in a sensational 110–100 win over Seattle, and he finished the season with a 24.2 average, seventh best in the league. He was also tenth in rebounding with 10.1 a game. Magic was a passing fool with 23 assists in a win over Seattle, including 12 in the first quarter, tying an NBA record set by Boston's Bob Cousy. He led the league in assists with 13.1 a game, and he was fifth in the league in steals with 2.24 per game.

But more than that—Magic and Bird had the attitude. No matter what happens in the final moments of the game, the ball is still bouncing and toes are still tapping. Magic put the attitude into his own words: "It's like 'Hey, when you come to play us, you're not going to get a win. You just better hope you come close.' That's playing loose."

Consequently, the NBA playoffs in 1984 were merely an opportunity to anticipate the ultimate match-up. Here, however, was also an opportunity to measure the stature of the 2 rising superstars. The Celtics blew by the Washington Bullets in the miniseries to open the playoffs, and as they went one-up on the New York Knicks in the Eastern Conference semifinals, Bird was still doing it all. What made him a winner was the ability to become stronger as the season became longer. Through the first 5 games of the playoffs, Bird led the Celtics in every statistical category except rebounding, in which he was second to Parish. He wasn't getting tired; he was getting better with 37 points on 16-for-22 shooting as

Boston went up 2 games on the Knicks. In the seventh and deciding game Bird scored his playoff high 39 points, as *New York Times* columnist Dave Anderson wrote on May 14, 1984, "from somewhere near the Bunker Hill monument."

Just when it seemed that they had done it all, the ability to go one better enabled Earvin and Larry to make the difference between winning and losing. The Lakers disposed of Dallas in the Western semis and Phoenix in the finals. In game 2 against Phoenix, Magic had his mates fighting for lay-ups as he dished off a playoff record 24 assists. He was unsurpassed. When Magic triggered an assault with cream pies on Wilkes in celebration of Jammal's thirtieth birthday, Magic hurled a cream pie right past Jammal and right at Kareem. After all, Kareem was open and Wilkes was already covered.

After Magic and company whipped the Suns, he realized the Celtics were about to down the Milwaukee Bucks in the Eastern finals. Magic watched Bird hit a 3-point play to tie the last game at 87, and as he hit off the drive to put the Celtics ahead for good, Magic screamed, "Oh, boy! Everybody wants it. The world wants it. Me and Larry at last."

The ramifications of this close encounter forced Larry and Magic to the forefront for a very good reason. "Their value transcends statistics," said Wilkes at the time. "Their personalities, their rivalries in college from the NCAA championship all help to make them somewhat larger than life."

The outcome would have even more impact. "Whoever wins, whatever team plays the best," said Pat Riley, "they will say that player had the most impact."

Now they were motivating each other. Magic was

already a winner with a pair of NBA titles, but think of how much would be added to his stature if he could win one more time against Larry. Bird already had a title, too, but here was the opportunity to prove he could beat Magic. Bird came out in the opening game, hit 7-for-17 from the field, and scored 24 very quiet points. Magic had 18 points and 10 assists as the Lakers took game one in the Garden, 115–109.

Now it was Magic's series to win or lose. Game 2 was close all the way. With 35 seconds left, Johnson's 2 free throws put the Lakers ahead 113–111. Kevin McHale missed a pair of foul shots for Boston, and Magic came up the court with the game in his hands. Magic was double-teamed. He passed off to Worthy. Worthy passed off errantly, and the Celtics' Gerald Henderson stole the ball and scored to tie the game. With 13 seconds left, Magic had the ball in the front court and was looking for the game-winning play. Seconds ticked off with each dribble. The clock ran out. The ball was still bouncing.

Magic had failed to make a game-winning play. He had failed to give it his best shot, or even his last shot. The Celtics won in overtime. It didn't matter that Magic dished out a championship series record of 21 assists in his team's game 3 out a championship series record of 21 assists in his team's game 3 victory—with 13 seconds left in game 4, Magic found himself in the same position. And with the same result. Bird's 15-foot jumper with 16 seconds left was the play that would be remembered in the Celtics 129–125 victory. Now it was Bird's series to win or lose. He scored 34 points with 17 rebounds in a game 6 win, after which Riley said, "Nothing seems to work on Bird. You could put him in a box, and he'd still pop out to get his points and rebounds.''

The Lakers clamped down on Bird in game 6 and held him to 8-for-11 from the field and 28 points. But after game 7 it was Magic who spent the post-game celebration in the shower, perhaps trying to wash off the disappointment. He had the ball stolen from him twice when the Lakers were within 2 points in the final minutes. Crunch time was supposed to be clutch time for Magic, but it was Larry who came through in the clutch with 20 points in the 111–102 victory for the Celtics.

''We made five mistakes that cost us the series, and I contributed to three of them,'' said Johnson, who then decided he would rather rave with a review of Bird, the playoff MVP. ''He's head and shoulders above everybody else.''

Words of encouragement for Magic came from the other locker room. Clearly Bird knew what it meant to have been able to take part in this moment with the Magic Man. ''He gets in the middle and makes things happen like nobody else in the league,'' Bird said of his counterpart. ''His game is perfect. He's a perfect player.''

No one could explain what Magic was feeling now. Riley tried. ''When you play the ultimate game, there's winning and there's misery. For Magic this was misery.''

Magic Johnson's ability to win, however, was now going to be defined by his inability to accept defeat. After the game, he was in the showers so long that Laker publicist Josh Rosenfeld became worried and went in after him. ''He and Michael Cooper were just sitting on the floor, all covered with soap, talking,'' he said.

That night, Magic rapped all night with Isiah Thomas and Mark Aguirre. Sleep would only induce the nightmare. For nights on end, Magic would close his eyes and see that last possession again and again. There was James Worthy open under the hoop, and still there was no way Earvin could get him the ball. "I'll be sitting somewhere and relaxing and here it comes right up in my mind," he later recalled. "I can still see Worthy open." So he went to his newly purchased Bel Air mansion and sat in the empty rooms and wondered about what went wrong.

The Press called him "Tragic" Johnson, and a headline in the Los Angeles Times asked, "Earvin, what happened to Magic?" He couldn't even talk to his mother or father about it. "I guess he was so filled with hurt," said Christine Johnson.

This is what made Magic Johnson a winner. He came back and led the Lakers to a rematch with the Celtics for the 1985 NBA championship. He also led the league in assists, not as a method to show people that he wasn't a loser but because that was all he could do to get the Lakers in position to win. Magic was still leading the league in assists; he even led in steals that season. He still came up with a triple double every third or fourth game. The last week of December provided some vintage Magic. On December 21, he had 25 points, 10 rebounds, and 12 assists in a 119–105 win over Phoenix, and a week later he had 12 points, 14 assists, and 11 rebounds in a 135–123 defeat of Denver. The next night Earvin had 15 points, 10 rebounds, and 16 assists in a 113–107 victory over the L.A. Clippers. Happy New Year.

The difference in his game was visible in a face only

a mother could read. "If you noticed, before when he was playing, he used to smile a lot," said Christine Johnson. "But now he doesn't smile as much. It's just a sign of his new determination. I see him settling down and becoming more of a man."

Part of being a winner means you're only as good as your last game. And part of Magic and Larry was to do whatever possible to make sure that last game was a victory. Take Bird, for example. After the 1984 season he was named the league's Most Valuable Player. He took the award home to French Lick, put it in a closet, and set out that summer to get even better. Was it possible for him to get any better?

In French Lick he worked as if he had been the one with soap in his eyes. He went down to the high school and worked out all morning with the weights he'd donated. Then he shot all afternoon. He sometimes worked until 7 P.M. There wasn't much time for golf that summer. There wasn't much time for anything besides working on his game and sleeping, the 2 things Larry likes to do more than anything else except, perhaps, drink beer.

"You've got to understand, basketball was never recreation for me. It was something I fell in love with. I spent maybe two weeks after the season was over not playing, but then I made the decision. I knew I had to take it upon myself to say, 'Okay guys, I came back in the best shape I've ever been in and I want it.' " With the start of the season, Bird's average was up to 27 points a game. He was shooting 92% from the foul line, and he was leading the league in 3-point shooting at a 48% clip, nearly twice his career average. And bird made it clear that the whole point to his dedication was not just to put up better numbers.

"I can't understand the guy who thinks he had a good game when he scores twenty-five points and his team loses. I don't understand that thinking at all. When I start accepting losing I'll get out."

In 1984 the Celtics were off to their best start ever. As Bird struck for 40 points in a 114–99 defeat of Dallas on December 10, the Celtics were 15–1. After he scored 48 points against Atlanta in a 128–127 victory, his average was up to 30.6. Later in the season he burned Atlanta for a career-high 60 points. The last player to score 60 points was Wilt, wasn't it? Or was it Russell? Anyway, the Celtics were now the winningest team in basketball, and given a strong chance of becoming the first team to win back-to-back titles since Bill Russell and the 1968–69 Celtics did it. Bird was perhaps becoming the ultimate winner.

"They both had a burning determination as far as being competitive," said Celtics' coach K.C. Jones, who was also a teammate of Russell's. "They've crossed the line. They have to win. You watch Larry and you see him diving after loose balls and getting floor burns and getting knocked under the boards and he still comes back for more. A guy like Larry gives the fan in the stands an idea of creativity and imagination most can't equal. He provides them entertainment, which is part of what this is all about."

To think that the low point of this season for Bird came on November 9, when he got into a fight with Julius Erving and they both were ejected! Reportedly, the officiating was at fault on a night when grabbing an opponent's uniform seemed to be within the rules. Bird was outscoring Erving 42–6 at the time, which may had something else to do with it, but the melee resulted in more than $30,000 in fines. Larry and the Doc eventually got together for an emotional apology, albeit a mutual one. The next time they squared off, they shook hands and came out exciting. Larry had 34 points to 16 for Erving; this made the fighting significant only because it happened when Bird had perhaps overcome Dr. J as a status symbol.

"His responsibility is larger than mine right now," Erving said. "Every night, they expect thirty points from him, and to be the leading rebounder. I've been in that situation—it's tough."

In the meantime, Earvin Johnson was most popular in the balloting for the All-Star Game, and at the very least that made him a winner with the fans. Who was better would again be decided in the NBA championship series, and Magic knew it as early as the beginning of February when he said, "I hope the Celtics enjoy the regular season, because in the end they know they will have to see us."

Just when it seemed like Larry and Magic did everything they could to ensure another victory for the Celtics or the Lakers, they had that knack for going out and doing a little something extra. On back-to-back nights in January, Bird beat Portland by hitting a fadeaway jumper from the left-hand corner as he was moving out of bounds. He was so deep on the base line that he had to arch the shot over the backboard, and he just beat the final buzzer. Imagine that shot—moving one way and shooting the other. To comprehend how hard this shot is, go out and try it. Or try to bank a running right-hander off the glass with 2 seconds left and your team down by a hoop. That is what Larry did the next night to beat Detroit by one point.

Only by realizing how difficult it is to do what these players did night after night are you able to best appreciate their propensity for success. And very few members of the media had to go that far to gain a proper perspective on Magic and Bird. Winners are people who don't stand by their past accomplishments. In fact, this more than anything else made Earvin and Bird winners. As the Celtics and Lakers were wrapping up their fourth Atlantic and Pacific Division titles respectively in the 5 years Johnson and Bird had been in the league, the line circumventing the world around each read: "This player, who no one thought could possibly improve, has actually gotten better."

As the 1985 playoffs hit the semifinal round, Bird found himself leaving a lasting impression on the professional basketball community. He had what arguably was his best season ever and was headed for a second straight MVP award, but in game 4 of the Eastern Conference semifinals against Detroit, he missed a shot that could have won the game. He went out the day before the next game and took 335 shots in practice. According to an observer, he made 274 of them. That is what it takes to be a winner. the Celtics disposed of Detroit, 4 games to 2, as Bird scored 43 points in the final victory. Beating the Sixers in the Eastern finals put the Celtics in the finals again, and put Bird in a position to establish himself as the ultimate winner.

Across the country, the Lakers were facing a must-win situation. Let it be known that Magic Johnson would prevail in such a situation. When L.A. was playing its best ball this season, the team was shooting well. And the team's shooting percentage skyrocketed in the playoffs. Magic was on top of his game and seemingly *above* the game, which enabled the Lakers to make easy shots. In the process of beating Denver 4 games to 1 in the Western finals, they hit 13 straight shots in game one, and they shot nearly 70% from the field in the first 4 games. In one particular 80-point half, Denver coach Doug Moe said, "I swear, I don't think they missed a shot. It's not bad enough you have to worry about Kareem and Worthy getting the ball inside. With magic in control, it seemed like everybody on their team was getting inside for easy buckets." This was the way Magic liked to win best.

As the 1985 NBA finals tipped off, the series was set to a rough-and-tumble tone. At this point, it seemed the only way to determine the winner would be by rumble. After Magic and Kevin McHale got into some pushing and shoving, Bird was up for it. "What we should do is just meet them out in the parking lot and have a fight to get it out of our systems. I don't know if the league is up for it, but the Celtics are."

The most memorable big picture from this series came as the Lakers went up 2 games to 1 with a 136–111 thrashing. There was Magic hovering over referee Earl Strom, while the Earl of Officiating was calling a technical foul against the Celtics. "Only one," said the Magic Man. Could it be he wanted to win *that* badly?

The Lakers won the series in 6 games, and that sixth game was a study in contrast; a regular role reversal from the previous spring. While Magic played, the Lakers fiddled with the Celtics; he had 14 points, 14 assists, and 10 rebounds in the 111–100 final victory. How appropriate it was that he ended with a triple double. Still, Magic's drive and determination to land this championship (rather than the actual accomplishment) that made him a winner.

"You wait so long to get back," he said. "A whole year, that's the hard part. But that's what makes this game interesting. It's made me stronger, better. You have to deal with different situations and see if you can come back. And, hey, I'm back."

Conversely, Bird scored 28 points in this final game, but it was on 12-for-29 shooting from the field. With that many shots, Bird was used to scoring 40 points, and he took the blame for the loss because, as he said, "I'm the type of guy who is supposed to bring us through, and I failed."

Only in the endeavor of the moment did he fail, however, and it wasn't long before Larry Bird showed the world how much of a winner he was. He answered every last question about his shortcomings in the final game, and when that was all over he stopped by the Lakers' locker room to offer congratulations.

In passing final judgment, it is best to accentuate the positive. Think of how much winning it took Earvin and Larry just to be facing each other. To get to the finals, not win, and then be judged a failure; that in itself is a no-win situation. Just being there year after year was the ultimate testimony to their winning ways.

7

What's In a Game

EVEN FOR LARRY BIRD AND MAGIC JOHNSON THERE WAS more to the game than highlights. They had been in the league for a mere 5 years, and already a wraparound bounce pass on the run or a falling, sprawling bank shot that rolled in even despite a foul on the play were just part of the game. Night after night, the great plays were becoming part of the routine. After each one, Larry would get up, bend down, and rub his hands on his sneakers. Magic would come back down the court, bobbing and weaving and smiling, and he would put his hand up for a high-five and yell, "Yeah, boy." It was all part of the game for Magic and the Bird.

Magic still had a smile on his face weeks after the Lakers won the 1985 NBA championship. He was on top of the world because he was on top of his game. It was indisputable, because he'd beaten Bird and the Celtics when Bird was on top of his game.

That great reference bible—the In-Your-Face Book of Basketball—devotes more than a few words to the karma of "game." When used as a proper noun, the term refers to the game of basketball, as in "Magic and Bird were the best in the game." There was another, more common usage particularly associated with Bird and Johnson: "They have taken the game into their own hands." When a player was on top of his game, he could shoot, pass, defend, rebound, and smile; he could do it all.

Your game is yours and only yours, because the elements involved are the moves only you can make, or because you make them in a way no one else does. Your game is something you always have. They can take away your ball, but they can never take away your game. And if they can take away your game, then your game isn't good enough. When Magic and Bird were playing so spectacularly midway through the 1980s, no one could take their game away.

Just what is in a game played by Magic or the Bird? Thee's more to it than mere highlights. The complete game involves dedication and preparation of extraordinary magnitude. That was perhaps the vital backbone for Magic's and Larry's game; all their movements stem from force of habit.

Natural talent, God-given ability, and other uncontrollable forces are not part of the concept; it's about attributes that are the result of hard work, the most inherent part of the game when it came to Magic and the Bird. Besides, if you were talking about God-given talent with either of these guys, there was their intelligence, soft hands, and perhaps good vision, though they have developed that last quality considerably, and not much else. And they're both also 6′ 9″.

For the most part what you saw was what they gave, 100 %, every night. The Magic Man always insisted that dedication was the mother of attention. He knew that making the people get up and dance was important to his game, so he worked on it during the off-season. Nothing ever happened on the spur of the moment with Earvin. "Magic's timing is always too good for chance," Paul Westhead said when he coached Johnson and the Lakers in 1980.

Look at the fourth game of the 1987 NBA championship series as an example. (A much closer look will follow.) The Lakers have come back from a 20-point deficit; with 15 seconds left, they had the ball and a one-point deficit. Magic took the in-bounds pass, dribbled across the lane, and lofted a soft hook shot right through the hoop to win the game. A clutch shot to be sure, but for Magic this was a no-risk situation. "He spent all last summer working on that shot," said Celtic guard Sam Vincent, who played college ball at Michigan State and spent his summers in East Lansing hooping with Johnson and his older brother, Jay Vincent. "You should see how many times he made it."

The point was well-taken. It seemed as though every summer Earvin went home and worked to add something to his game. He relentlessly worked on his intensity and his stamina. For several summers Magic, Isiah Thomas, and Mark Aguirre put together a barnstorming all-star team that traveled the country playing exhibitions. Practice made perfect, and Johnson was never satisfied on any of these nights unless he left the crowd standing on its feet.

After one game in the middle of winter, Earvin was sitting at his locker talking with some reporters about the importance of intensity, emotion, and enthusiasm in regards to the Lakers' fast break. "You know the best part is that the crowd gets going, and it's ooooh, we're gone."

Wouldn't it be great if there was a story about how Magic went home to Lansing every summer, and he played and worked and played some more until he had improved all the weaknesses in his game? Yes, it would, but that is Larry's story, and anyway, Magic spent so much time practicing and shooting and working on all phases of his play that he came into the NBA with very few flaws in his game. Instead, much of his effort off the court was devoted to cerebral preparation. Magic would sit by the pool at his Bel Air mansion and think about all the possibilities. He had unique physical attributes; he was quick and at 6' 9" he towered over the rest of the league's point guards. Magic came to training camp each fall prepared to flaunt those assets to the Lakers' advantage. And he would prove that his possibilities were endless.

Bird took the long road to training camp, the uphill one all the way. Part of Bird's ritual during the summer was to run up the glorious hills of southern Indiana, which is probably what enabled him to make the one last-ditch effort to save a loose ball going out of bounds. And it doesn't seem too farfetched an idea to compare making it to the top of the hill with out-hustling everybody else in the final minutes of the fourth quarter of an NBA game. Bird spent more time on those hills the summer after he won his first MVP award, and Celtics' general manager Jan Volk noticed the difference. "If you'd had told me at the end of last season, he was going to play better this year I'd have been amazed. But he has played better. Perhaps it's because of the time he spent running up those hills in the summer.'' Walter Payton used to spend his summers running up a hill in back of his house in suburban Chicago, and for 14 years he was considered the best football player in the game. Apparently staying on top of your game is sometimes an uphill battle.

There was more to it than that, of course Bird spent his mornings lifting weights, and the afternoons playing tennis with Dinah, or golf. And he made sure to get plenty of rest. But aside from height and big, soft hands, Bird never had much else to go on. He was ambidextrous off the court; he used his left for eating and writing. But with Larry, it was not hard to think that perhaps he worked on developing that talent along with the rest of the package.

Bird was one of those rare talents who could put in a full day's work on the court all by himself. Practice for the day had just finished for Celtics, and so it was time for Bird to go to work. Before he even picked up the ball, he jumped rope for, 5 minutes to loosen up. This is how *his* game was played.

He dropped the rope, and slapped the ball up from the floor as if he were bringing it to life. He pranced about the gym, working the ball on the dribble, between his legs, around his back, in front, in back. He went to his left; he went to his right. He threw the ball off the wall or off a door, and it came back to him. Watch Bird in any game and notice the ball always comes back to him.

The routine continued with lay-ups, hook shots, short

jumpers. He shot from each spot in sets of 10; there
were no misses. Bird then proceeded to go around his
world by hitting jump shots from one side of the court
to the other. He moved out from 15 feet to 20 feet and
shot his way back to the other side. The ball would hit
nothing but net and bounce right back to him. Then he
shot of the dribble, turning around, from the corner,
over his head, from 3-point land, from beyond. In this
practice Larry Bird took every shot he could think of.

Of all the players he faced, no one could challenge
Larry Bird like Larry Bird. "Being out there alone . . .
I've always liked it best that way. At midnight, like
that, when it's really quiet, or early in the morning
when there's nobody else around." This is why Larry
Bird could walk into any situation in any game and
make it look as if he were playing in his own little
world.

Perhaps there is no more dedicated a player than
Bird, who even devoted much effort to working on his
comprehension of the game. Nobody better understood
how to play defense as illegally as the rules would
allow. In the NBA, teams must play man-to-man defense, and so there must always be at least one man on
one man unless 2 or 3 come over to help guard the ball,
which is usually the case with Magic and Bird. A player
who drops too far off his man and into a zone on the
floor is playing illegal defense. It was as if Bird measured the distance he could legally drop off, for he
knew that could put him in better position to clog a
passing lane or steal the ball or wreak whatever havoc
possible.

Bird was a true student of his game. He went on
record with long, in-depth theories of rebounding. When

you're 6' 9", and can't jump, you have to make a science of it to be good at it. As Herbert Warren Wind wrote in the *New Yorker*, "Bird has the knack for reading where a rebound will go. All he has to see is a couple of yards of the ball's parabola to have a good idea of where the ball will strike the backboard, the rim of the basket, or both, and where it is likely to come down. This accounts for the high number of rebounds he gets even though there are taller players and more remarkable jumpers."

As hard to believe as it would seem, there was still more to Larry and Magic's game than that. In fact, the way they went about preparation, there was more to their games than the game itself. For them, the game always began long before they took the court.

Larry Bird liked to take the first shot of every game. And if he made it, he would bend down and rub his hands on his shoes, and he'd probably spend the rest of the night doing both right in the opposition's face. K.C. Jones said this was part of Bird's "instinctive work ethic," a quality making Bird so relentless in his preparation.

On game day, he was always the first one to arrive at the stadium. If he was going to the Garden, the same man would meet him at the front door and take his car. In front of any empty arena Bird played his best game. He would start in one corner and shoot his way around to the other corner, pausing only for free throws. He started from 20-feet out and moved into the 10-foot mark to practice the short jumpers which "can make the difference in the game." He rushed himself just enough to simulate the game condition of having to hurry a shot, and in the heat of this personal competition he made sure to slow himself down and practice putting the shot up with just the right touch in the midst of chaos. Sometimes a ball boy would be out there to rebound, but then Bird rarely needed the rebounder. The ball always seemed to find its way back to Bird's hand. This wasn't much different from the ritual he used at practice, but Bird's game-day shoot-arounds were legendary.

"You see," Larry explained, "I enjoy the game to the point where even though I have teammates, I sometimes wish I could be like Jimmy Connors in tennis and not have to worry about all the guys getting fired up and just be out there by myself and see what I could do. Sometimes when things aren't going too good, and everyone seems down and everyone is on our butt, that's when you say, 'Damn it, let me go out there and get 'em. I'll bust 'em. Let me go one-on-one.' "

The hardest part of Larry Bird's game to understand was how he could come out to start the game and immediately catch fire from the field. When you warm up that much, you better be hot. But it was interesting to note that in his first MVP season, Bird put in an extra half-hour of pre-game shooting. He has done that ever since.

Bird, however, had another way of getting up for his game. "There were some times when I would get up in the morning, and say, 'Oh no, not another game.' I'll stay that way until the national anthem is over with and they throw the ball up, and then I have so much fun and I enjoy myself out there so much that everything else goes out the window." When they would strike up the band in the Garden for the national anthem, Bird immediately gazed toward the heavens. (Looking at all the championship banners to fill himself with Celtic pride, no doubt.)

Actually, what Bird was doing was looking at the banner bearing the retired number 4 of the Boston Bruins great Bobby Orr. He has fixed upon that number so long and so many times, he can recreate it from memory. He knows every stitch; he even knows how many lines pierce the circle on the capital B of the banner. "Eight," Larry said. "Don't bet me on it."

Even when a game was over, it wasn't over for Bird. Part of his success came from being able to put the present game out of his mind when it's over and concentrate on the one ahead. Consequently, even though Bird was the first to arrive, he was always the last to leave. He stayed in the showers the longest in order to give his teammates adequate play with the media, and he would meet the press only when all of that was over so he would only have to answer each question just once.

Magic Johnson spent little of his game days thinking about the night's event. Remember that night in 1980 when he scored 42 points to lead the Lakers to the NBA championship, the night when he was Kareem for a day. With everything riding on the line, the spunky 20-year-old never gave any of it a second thought. "When I got to the hotel," he recalled, "I hopped in my bed, told the operator to hold the calls, took my box, turned on my tunes, and jammed. And dreamed up a little bit of the game."

Before Earvin Johnson ever stepped onto the court to become the Magic Man, he would get himself into the right mood by being the music man. This was when he would turn into the E. J. the Deejay, the man who picks the tunes to make the rest of boys rock 'n' roll. And you know about all the time Earvin spent as a kid practicing to be a lead singer.

"You play to a beat, on a stride," said the ultimate maestro. "Sometimes if I have been listening to a song, it will come up in my mind during a game. I always listen to music before a game. It gets me going, pumps my blood up. I'll always be more sweaty when I leave home than I am after warmups. I'm thinking about the game, but I'm into the music. You get too uptight if you're thinking about the game all day. It's there, but I'm not focused in on it. Cool. By the time I hit my car, I want an up beat, because by then my adrenaline's flowing."

Rhythm and blues put Magic in his game rhythm. Jeffrey Osborne was cool; so was Luther Vandross. For a big game the featured artist may have been the Parliament Funkadelic. And that is why Magic was always so much like music and motion. He would come out for the opening tip, having already been rocking and rolling. When he really had the music in him and his energy was flowing freely from it, well, those were the nights when Earvin never missed a beat. And whether Magic was singing a victory song in the end or signing the blues, the night of a home game always ended with an extended stay in the Jacuzzi of his master bedroom, where he could stare out the window and tune in to the next endeavor.

When Magic was really in tune with the rhythm of his game, he could turn any play into a riff of beautiful improvisation. In the May 13, 1985, issue of *Sports Illustrated*, writer Bruce Newman described such a moment when Magic was so into his game that he was pounding to the beat of a different drum than anyone else on the floor. As Newman wrote, "During a game at Kansas City in March, he warmed up with a first-quarter fast break on which he was met by a defender at the free-throw line. He dribbled behind his back without breaking stride and dished to Cooper for a lay-up. In the fourth quarter, he came charging down the floor on a break when a defender again stopped him at the foul line. He pirouetted 360 degrees and glided in on stride to the basket. At courtside, Lakers' radio announcer Chick Hearn said, 'God and all his apostles could not have stopped that move.' "

Beyond his ability to rebound with the big guys and run the floor with the little guys and score with any guy, there always seemed to be something special about Magic's game. He called this sixth sense *court sense*. "My whole game is court sense, being smart, taking charge, setting up a play if I have to or scoring."

When Magic was playing his game at its best, he was playing all the angles. He used his size and quickness to move by his defender and challenge the big guys on defense. By inducing the defender to move up and play him, Magic thereby created a diagonal between himself and a teammate. Basketball linguists called this a passing lane, for the shortest distance to the basket was this straight line. "If I can hit that seam and find the angle, somebody can take the pass and shoot without breaking stride. It's just like shooting pool: You have to antici-pate what's going to happen, read the angle, then pow. It just happens."

Magic said he tried to pattern his game after Dr. J and George "Iceman" Gervin, the coolest scorer in the game in his day. Magic liked their style because they were, as he said, "smoooooth." Magic had that ability to score in big bunches, but he was able to do so much more with the basketball. He passed blindly better than anybody. Hearn said he remembered more than a few times when Magic looked up at the ceiling of the Forum and hit Worthy right in stride with a scoring pass.

Then again, the best part of Magic's game wasn't always easy to explain. He'd get that look that seemed to say "Full speed ahead," and in a minute the Lakers were running over the opposition. Because he's 6' 9", he could crash the defensive boards and snare the rebound. And because he's a guard he saved the team the trouble of throwing the outlet pass to trigger the fast break. Instead, Magic was the team's outlet; he would take the ball off the boards and run it up the court himself.

Yet the ability to know just when to jack it up and kick it out may have been the most fascinating part of Earvin's game.

"Something in my head tells me to take over," Johnson said in 1985 when the Lakers were breaking right on stride in the championship series against the Celtics. "I can see it spread to the rest of the Lakers after we run the break a few times. We're getting the feeling we can't be stopped. It's a feeling inside. Things start happening so fast, there's nothing the defense can do to stop us."

How about a few from the other side? What was it like to see Magic and the Lakers coming at you on the break? What did an opponent think the best part of Earvin's game was, the toughest part to take away? "The thing about magic is that he just does what he wants to," said Jim Paxson in 1985 when he was playing with Portland. "He can score six points and totally dominate a game, which he's done against us. Or he can decide they need points and go out and score thirty-nine, which he's also done against us. He just reads the flow of the game and decides what he's going to do that night.''

Perhaps it was more than the mannerisms that were telltale signs of a night to remember for Magic or the Bird. It was plain to see the smile, or Larry bending down to rub his sneakers, but that was probably only a gesture to pay homage to his high-tops. When Bird played his game as best as he could, he would leave people speechless.

Out on the break, Bird was open but the lead pass was thrown too far ahead and seemed to be headed out of bounds. But just then Bird would dive and throw the ball back over his shoulder to hit Kevin McHale right in stride to the hole. *Oooooh*. More often than not it was difficult to put Bird's game into words.

''It's savvy or something,'' said one-time teammate Dave Cowens. ''Larry's got it. Something mental that other players with more physical talent don't have.''

On the other hand, Danny Vranes, one of the NBA's best defensive forwards in the 1980s, knew exactly what Cowens was talking about. ''It's no mystery why he is so good,'' said Vranes who, while playing with the Seattle Supersonics, was always assigned to defend Bird. ''He may not look like a Rhodes scholar out there, but he is two steps ahead of everyone else in his thinking. The guy's feel for the game and his offensive imagination are so far advanced it's ridiculous.''

The book on Bird was that he did see the game a play or 2 ahead of everyone else. To put it another way, while everyone else saw the game at regular speed, he played it in slow motion. Experts who followed the other winter game—the one played on ice—also said that about Wayne Gretzky, the undisputed greatest hockey player to ever play that game. *Time* magazine once said that about both Bird and Gretzky in the same story. The fact of the matter is indisputable: His vision was astounding; he was forever able to spot friends sitting way up in the bleachers at Boston Garden.

Bird's vision is what set up the rest of his game. He had the whole package, as they used to say. He could take the ball to the hoop to his right or left. He could shoot hook shots and short jumpers with his right hand or his left hand. He could move out to the perimeter and beyond and hit with his right hand or his left hand. He could do it all that on the run as well.

Bird would bring the ball into the front court and be able to slow down and watch the defense and offense set up. He reacted to the play, and because he could pass either way with either hand, he was too talented to defend one-on-one or even two-on-one. He made the defense second-guess him: Would he drive, would he pass, would he pop the jumper? He was always a split second ahead of the game.

Remember the way Larry used to take the ball off the board, turn, and throw a touchdown-like outlet pass to Danny Ainge way down court? Remember the great one he threw in game 4 of the 1987 NBA finals? He was falling back out of bounds, and he hurled a left-hand bullet that hit Ainge right in stride. *Oooooh*. It was his ability to see the opportunity for the outlet developing before everyone else and then get the pass off that made the play.

This could go on forever. Bird had guile and he used

the art of deception to beat the opposition. He knew exactly what move each of his teammates would make as he stood with his back to the defense, waiting to make something happen. He had great hand-eye coordination, which he also used quite efficiently on the golf course and the tennis court whenever he had the opportunity. He knew his game, and he knew the game. He knew as well as Magic what the game was like when it was great, *really* great.

"It makes you feel great when you play a good game," said the Bird. "It gives you a great sense of gratification. Sometimes, I really believe I'm playing so well no one can guard me."

Sports Illustrated's master wordsmith, Frank DeFord, tried to describe Bird's game in a March 21, 1988, feature. "Larry Bird remains, simply Larry. He seems merely the sum of little bits—a bit more clever than you and me, a bit more dedicated, a bit better on his shooting touch, a bit better with . . . but certainly nothing out of the ordinary. Larry Bird is like when you first learn fractions and you have to change everything to twelfths to make it possible to add up the thirds and fourths and sixths. All the other great players are so obviously whole numbers."

There were players who could rebound, shoot, and pass like Magic and Bird. Well, they could shoot and rebound like Larry and Earvin. But no one ever did it all so well at the same time. In the 1980s, basketball's popular culture created a statistic with which to measure all-around play. About the same time, the concept of a triple double became a common description of the way Bird and Johnson played the game.

In college, Magic and Bird probably didn't even

know what they had accomplished with triple doubles. In the pro game, Magic came up with a triple double every fourth game or so. In his MVP season of 1986–1987 Magic came close to averaging a triple double. Though 1988, Bird had 52 career triple doubles. In December of 1984, Bird put together 3 straight triple doubles. In the 1986 playoffs, he had another 3 in a row.

And that's what was in the game for Magic and the Bird. That was why their game was one and the same, a combination, a process. The rebounding went along with the passing and the scoring. Defense was a part of the big picture. Sometimes the biggest play of the game came on defense, when Bird would watch a player jump by him to the hole, while he would sneak in from the back and block the shot. Timing was everything. Magic had a knack for stepping up into a passing lane to make a steal and take the ball out on the break without even breaking stride. What Magic and Bird had really done was to take the game into their own, very capable hands.

8

What's In a Name

THE MOMENT HE WALKED IN THE JOINT EARVIN JOHNSON was a man of distinction. The way he filled the room always made him a popular face in the crowd, which on any given night might have included Jack Nicholson or Michael Jackson or any of his other close friends. He always had a lot of close friends, because the way Johnson brought out the best in people was simply Magic.

When Christine Johnson first heard her son called "Magic," she considered it blasphemy. That was back in 1977, when a sportswriter in East Lansing, Michigan, used the term to describe what Earvin could do with basketball. In college it was Earvin "Magic" Johnson, and when he made it to the pro game it was simply Magic.

"Magic" was the man in the NBA. Magic was the guy who laughed and jived and went on television with

Brent Musburger and said, "Hi y'all. Big game today. We gonna get after it. Try to make it *eeeasy*." He was one of *People* magazine's "25 most influential people"; he was the ultimate people person. When he walked into the room, chances were he would greet Michael Jackson or Muhammed Ali, or better yet, Janet Jackson, and then he would wind up talking hoops for the rest of the night with Bruce Willis. Magic was always up, out, and about, moonlighting around town.

Sitting in his Jacuzzi, though, at his beautiful Bel Air home, or walking down the streets of his neighborhood in Lansing with his namesake, he never had to be Magic. Even in his quietest moments, the homeboys knew him as E.J. or Junior, or if they needed a nickname it was "June Bug," or just plain "Bug." As in, "Hey Bug, you want to go play some hoop?" And then there was the side of Johnson that enabled him to run the show. He liked to call this character E.J. the Deejay; he was the guy who made sure everybody moved on the same beat. Songs were the key to life to E.J. the Deejay.

"Usually, I'm up, and people see me as up," Johnson said. "But people don't know me, really. I'm a quiet person who likes to have a lot of time to himself. Sometimes when you want to get away from that crowd, that's when you don't want to be Magic at all."

Whoever walked onto the court wearing number 32 for the Lakers was able to make an impression on people. Those who watched him closely and knew him best had a handle on the different sides of the man. "His appeal is universal," said Mitch Kupchak when he played with Johnson on the 1984–86 Lakers. Added former teammate Norm Nixon, "A lot of people think they know him from seeing him out or seeing him play. But they don't."

Pat Riley seemed to coach the Lakers according to which side of Johnson came to play. When they all came to play, he didn't have to coach at all. It wasn't hard to be a one-man team when there were so many of him. "Some nights when he plays, it's frivolity—footloose and fancy free. That's Magic," Riley reasoned. "Earvin is fundamental; it's substance, roots, family, and character."

There is room for all of Earvin Johnson in his 5-bedroom, 5-bath party haven in Bel Air. Modest by neighborhood standards, the house is home for all of Earvin's dreams. like the basketball court or the stereo console, the place is filled with aspects of his lifestyle.

The personal touch came from the good taste which is so much a part of Earvin, just plain "Junior" to his mother. Christine Johnson has a room in the house all her own. "I thought it was a good idea to make certain people comfortable when they come to visit." Earvin reasoned. "So I did it like they do in the fancy hotels. Three rooms are named after people for whom they have been reserved. There's the Christine Room, the Isiah Room, and the Tucker room."

The tucker room is particularly indicative of Earvin's personality. Dr. Charles Tucker is Earvin's close friend from Lansing and his personal confidant, a guy he rarely made a move off the court or the dance floor without consulting. Tucker's fond of antiques, so the Tucker Room in Bel Air is decorated with antique furniture. "Magic chose everything in the house himself," Tucker pointed out.

The other part of the house Earvin liked most was the Jacuzzi. After a game he could be alone there with his thoughts. "This is one of the best parts of the house," he said. "I had always dreamed of having a sunken-in tub since I saw one on a Camay commercial on TV. The girl goes through some big white pillars like she's in a castle, and then she comes walking out of this sunken-in bathtub. So sharp. When things are on my mind I come here a lot."

Earvin Johnson liked the simple things, even if that meant staying up late and watching television for 8 hours or going to the movies with the guys on the team. "It's funny sometimes, eight giants all sitting in a row at the movies." Earvin Johnson appeared on the *Tonight Show* with Johnny Carson every time the Lakers won the NBA title, and he was just a little bit nervous and, if you can believe it, camera shy. But the simple things to Earvin were spending time with the family, and even enjoying his solitude.

"I miss the community, the homeyness of it," Earvin said after 5 years of living in Los Angeles. "There everybody knows each other. You call people up, and in five minutes you got a softball game together. I like that; I miss it. I'm a family man."

Family made him feel good. After he had the knee operation that kept him out for 3 months in 1980–81, Paul Westhead went to the hospital to look in on Earvin. "I figured I'd go and find out what this guy was really like. So I went to the room and the door was closed and I thought, 'Aha! A sign.' I pushed the door open and there was Magic propped up in the bed with a Dodger cap on backward, a piece of apple pie shoved up under his face, watching a football game, yelling at his father and a bunch of friends playing cards to keep the noise down. I couldn't believe it.''

Earvin was perhaps most comfortable at home, where he could sit back and, as he said, ''be me. I don't have to worry about smiling or anything.'' Earvin was also the sensitive side of the man, more sensitive to the little things that made him happy. Earvin never hesitated to make it perfectly clear what was important.

Earvin knew the importance of being there to lend a helping hand. So he organized the league's greatest stars in 1985 to play a benefit game for the United Negro College Fund. ''A Midsummer Night's Magic'' was the event of the summer. A black-tie dinner was part of the festivities and the organization raised more than $500,000 in 1987.

Magic also went on the road to benefit what he deemed the most worthy of causes. He showed up in Chicago to play in the Operation PUSH/EXCEL all-star game on the same team with Mark Aguirre, Isiah Thomas, and Dominique Wilkins. They scored 187 points; Magic had too many assists to count. The only man who didn't get one of his no-look passes on this night was Jesse Jackson.

He also organized the players in the 1985 NBA All-Star Game to the Interaction Ethiopian Fund to help fight starvation in Africa. Closer to home, ''The Magic Show,'' costarring Isiah and Aguirre, played in Memphis, Tennessee, in 1985 to benefit ''USA for Africa'' and the residents in the hunger-ridden community of Tunica, Mississippi. Tunica was the hometown of Dr. Charles Tucker.

''Just doing our part to help out,'' Johnson said. His

part also included sponsoring a tutoring program in Lansing for children with reading difficulties. And how many times have you turned on the television and seen Earvin telling all the kids, "Don't foul out. Say no to drugs." He regularly toured Los Angeles schools delivering the same message. Earvin didn't need basketball to tell him how lucky he was to be alive. Living is what Earvin liked best.

"When I get up in the morning I'm grateful to see the sun. I'm just going to go on being happy old Earvin because that's what people seem to like. And it's fun to be liked, the funnest thing of all."

When Earvin was young, he spent most of his time hooping. When Earvin got older he spent most of his time hooping. But with all the hours on the court he couldn't go it alone. So Earvin took the radio with him, cranked up the tunes, and jammed for hours at a time. The bigger Earvin got, the bigger the radio he brought. And there he was playing one-on-one with himself: Earvin "Junior" Johnson vs. E.J. the Deejay.

The deejay is the man who gets the party going. As Magic once said, "He's the man who keeps everyone happy," the one who could always make the Los Angeles Forum rock and roll. Sometimes E.J. thought he could keep his teammates happy by singing along with his Walkman in the middle of Los Angeles International Airport. Nixon said he was much more moving on the court. He not only made the Lakers run and gun; he made them have fun along the way. Enthusiasm, exuberance, and effort each were vital parts of the team, and E.J. was the one responsible for turning up the volume. He spread the ball around so each teammate could take his best shot, and he made sure he got down and got tough when it was time to take care of business.

"The first thing he brought to us was a lot more excitement and enthusiasm," said former Lakers coach Jack McKinney, "and I think that was infectious. Also, when you have a player as heralded as he was, it helps if he spends all night trying to pass the ball to his teammates."

E.J. the Deejay was at home working the tools of his trade. The party room in the Bel Air pad was better equipped than most of L.A.'s best discos, with 40 colored stage lights hanging from the ceiling. This was E.J's favorite part of the house, the place where he could stand behind the console, play the tunes, and make the lights move in time with the music. There was a stereo speaker in every room of the house. There was even a speaker in the master bathroom. "I had the party area specially designed so I could continue as E.J. the Deejay," he confirmed with a smile so big it was more of a grin.

The rest of the house is simply Magic. He had an indoor basketball court built in, perhaps in case he ever wanted to bring his work home. One of the backboards in the court was made vertically mobile so the court could be used for raquetball and volleyball. And the magic touch was the 18-foot glass wall from which people in the party room could watch the activities on the court. What separated Magic from the other faces of his personality was style. Magic did everything in style.

A more credible source of reference—the *American Heritage Dictionary*—defines magic as, among other things, "any quality that seems to enchant." With that in mind, there are some things about Johnson you never realized could be magic. When Johnson would run downcourt not quite at full speed he sort of chugged along. He kind of waddled and at the same time he smiled, all of which helped to make every game part of some enchanted evening. It was like the way he talked. Every answer came down to 1 or 2 words. What was it like to run the fast break? "The ball comes off the board," said Magic. "It's out, and we're gone."

Magic was the side of Earvin that touched people, that made him memorable, that gave him his charm. One day in 1985 Earvin let Lon Rosen, director of promotions for the fabulous Forum, borrow his Mercedes while Rosen's car was in the shop. Rosen was out driving, "when suddenly something under the hood exploded." Rosen called up Earvin to tell him, and what was his response?

"Were you able to save the phone number that was in the glove compartment?"

Rosen responded, "Earvin, listen to me. Your forty-thousand-dollar car is in the middle of the street. It's toast. But all he kept asking was, Did you save that phone number?' " That was most definitely a magic moment.

"I don't know, I guess I have been blessed," Magic reasoned. "The strength comes from my father, the smile comes from my mother and . . . well, I just don't know why it's me. It just is. But it was always me. It goes all the way back to first grade."

Even back then, Magic was not only what he did on the basketball court. But that was the place where the magic was so inspiring. The impact was, perhaps, most readily seen when Johnson first came to play with the Lakers. As the Lakers' general manager Jerry West recalled, ''There were just rivers of emotion coming out of him. He was all over the place, smiling, laughing, jumping up and down after every basket.''

Magic was the part of the man who loved to play the game and could play it nonstop. Magic was when he would fire a pass between two defenders to a teammate so buried in traffic that he didn't think he was open. The ball made it through into the hands of the unsuspecting teammate, who might have been Jim Chones, Jammal wilkes, or James Worthy. It was an optical illusion—or so it seemed.

''He really is magic,'' Brian Taylor of the San Diego Clippers said after the first time he played against Johnson in 1980. ''He's got great charisma. It's just fun to watch someone who can get the ball to his teammates when they're open. There are a few other players who can do that, but what makes Magic magic is the way he brings his personality to it.''

Magic was most visible in public because that was who people wanted to see. Magic would come to a friend's party, and the first thing he would do was to pay his respects to every guest before helping himself to something to eat. But when Earvin became so magical, the stars came out to see him. He heard Bruce Willis was at a party, and he was excited to talk to him about his hit television show *Moonlighting*. ''But he only wanted to talk about basketball,'' Magic said. ''So you should have seen us, like two kids sitting on the couch talking the night away.''

Magic's appeal is so vast that Eddie Murphy and Michael Jackson often called him to see what was happening or to see if the Magic Man might want to go out and party that night. Darwin Payton, a close friend, used to accompany Magic out on the town. He was able to see why Earvin was filled with so much magic.

"A lot of people treat him like he's supernatural because of the way he played," Payton said. "I've been with him in a lot of places, and wherever he is, he's the man. When he was at a club, the stars all came over to see him."

Magic had become a star. He almost made an episode of the since-cancelled television series *The White Shadow*, starring Ken Howard as a former pro player who became a high school basketball coach. He did other television shows, and he was a natural in commercials. He even made one for Converse with Larry Bird right there on the court in Bird's backyard. And at the height of his career, it was virtually impossible to cruise the streets of Los Angeles without seeing magic holding up a can of 7-Up or telling people "Buick is better." His commercial appeal was magical, and Earvin worked hard at it. Directors loved to work with him, for he wouldn't leave the set until he had taken care of business. "Are you sure you got it?" he asked. "Did you get my good side?"

The Magic Man was, by his own reckoning, a fun man. "That's the me who does whatever I feel like on instinct. It might be watching TV for seven or eight hours, it might be going to the park just walking and thinking, it might be going where some kids are and watching them. Whatever comes to my mind, whatever gives me some fun."

That was the Magic *People* magazine made one of its "25 Most Influential People of 1987." That was the Magic who, upon hearing that advice columnist Ann

Landers had attended a game featuring the lowly Chicago Bulls in 1984, said, "She must have some problems of her own." That was the Magic would would go to a Madonna concert and laugh at the way some of the teenage girls were dressed, and then he'd wind up dancing alongside them in the aisles.

Earvin "Magic" Johnson is one of the few men in the world who could be his own dancing partner.

9

Talk Is Cheap

IF YOU COULDN'T REACH OUT AND TOUCH LARRY BIRD, then wouldn't long distance be the next best thing to being there? Since we know everybody who knows anything about the game has something to say about Larry Bird, wouldn't it be nice if we could all sit around and listen to what everybody is talking about? Imagine if the quickest way to get the last word on Larry Bird would be to dial direct; a 900-number could bridge the gap between all the Bird men and women all around the nation. If you're a Bird fan, just call: 1–900–BIRD–MAN. This will be your opportunity to hear just what all Bird fans are talking about. And on the party line at any given time of the day you just might catch Kevin McHale, Julius Erving, Dominique Wilkins, Isiah Thomas, Magic Johnson, perhaps even Red Auerbach or any of the rest of his fans rapping on the Bird.

When the subject was what could be done to stop Larry Bird, former Drake University basketball coach Bob Ortegel was the first to speak up. "What do you take away from Larry Bird? How about his sneakers."

So how good *is* Larry Bird? Scotty Robertson, long-time NBA head coach and assistant coach, said: "He's so damn good, he's making a farce of the game."

Portland coach Jack Ramsay added, "He's the greatest clutch player of all time."

Artis Gilmore remarked: "Larry Bird is a unique phenomenon."

"I think that Larry is a very, very good basketball player," said Isiah Thomas in a controversial remark, "but I'd have to agree with [Dennis] Rodman. If Bird was black, he'd be just another good guy."

Bird's response was: "I don't think Isiah meant it as a racist remark. I like Isiah. I still like Isiah."

If there can also be a Larry Bird Ford-Lincoln Mercury dealership complete with a parquet floor, then why not a 900-number to talk to Larry Bird? It would only be one of the many ways Bird junkies could find their fix. After all, it is a long way for most to travel to Terre Haute to see Larry Bird's Boston Connection Hotel, where a satellite dish beams in Celtic games to the Bird's Nest Sports Lounge. There you can get a bite to eat in the MVP Club dining room or the Boston Garden Family Restaurant, where miniature championship banners hang from the ceiling and the placemats are actual-size reproductions of Larry Bird's hands. If there are Larry Bird golf balls, which there are, Larry Bird shower curtains, Larry Bird playing cards (he's the joker), Larry Bird chocolates, and Larry Bird coloring books for the young fan in the family, why not a Larry Bird network for mass communication?

Imagine what it would be like to be able to talk with Bird. His agent, Bob Woolf, once thought he had an important phone conversation with Larry.

"I have three things to talk to you about," Woolf began. "The president of Harvard would like you to address the freshman class."

"No," Larry said emphatically.

"*Sports Illustrated* wants you to pose for a cover."

"No."

"*Life* magazine wants to do a photo essay on you, but . . ."

"No. Mr. Woolf. I thought you said this was an important call."

That's Larry. Perhaps it was the beloved and betrothed Dinah Mattingly who put it best when she said that to know Larry is to love him, or something to that effect.

What Dinah has put up with beyond the many hours of rebounding in the process of loving Larry. . . . The most famous incident concerning Dinah and Larry has to have been the one night they went to a drive-in movie. Dinah went to get popcorn and drinks, and while she was gone, Larry moved his pickup truck to another space. She came back and the car wasn't there. Larry tooted the horn and she went in that direction. Then someone else honked his horn, and then the whole place was tooting. Dinah was left standing in frustration holding the bag of popcorn.

After years of listening to Larry ask, "Why ruin a good relationship by getting married," one night during the winter of 1988, Dinah watched as Larry leaned across the front seat of his Ford Bronco, held out a diamond ring, and said to her, "You can wear this if you want to." Dinah joked with friends that Larry finally gave her the ring only after his pet Doberman, Klinger, died.

One time the Boston *Herald American* called to do an article on Larry as one of the city's most eligible bachelors. Nobody ever talked much about the commercial he made for Chardon jeans. He was a fan of Kenny Rogers's music, and for a good meal he like to go out for Italian food. That's about it for gossip.

Bird probably surpassed some of Boston's greatest athletes in his popularity. There was Bird, and then there was Bobby Orr, Carl Yazstremski, Carlton Fisk, and, with all due respect, Ted Williams. Woolf had testimony to such a fact in the form of a file cabinet full of "Larry Bird stuff" in his office. And Larry was the only man in town whose actions were put into music. On their record, "The Bird Rap," Li'll Davey B and the Space Kadettes sang about Larry's game—"so well-rounded it is almost absurd."

It seemed as though Larry Bird could always inspire originality. A lot of the scuttlebutt concerning the Bird Man was pretty much the same. Anybody who knew anything about the game wanted to be heard on the matter of how great a player he was. There are even those who would go beyond saying that Bird was the best forward to ever play the game or that he was the best white basketball player. When the topic of conversation was how to defend Larry Bird, well, only a few brave men ever cared to comment. But when the subject was Larry Bird, his closest friends and competitors couldn't wait to run off at the mouth.

"I'd pay to watch him play," Magic Johnson said.

Kevin McHale had no problem agreeing with that

sentiment. "Hey, Larry Bird is like Elvis," he said. "He's the king."

The Bird Man never minded being the butt of a good joke, and he was always one for a good laugh. But he was the source of amusement for so many fans. Nobody ever had a problem laying it on Larry. That was the way they talked about him—in perpetual one-liners.

Remember the play in the 1981 championship series against Houston when Bird followed his own missed shot from the top of the key, caught the rebound on the base line, and hit a hanging jump shot with his left hand? The play that Red Auerbach called the greatest he'd ever seen? Houston forward Billy Paultz had his own point of view on the effort: "Julius Erving . . . he he makes dramatic plays. He hits the home run. Larry Bird . . . he hits the triple. That play was a triple. A triple is enough to win in this league."

Dominique Wilkins said, "Look into his eyes and you see a killer." Celtic teammate and assistant coach Chris Ford added, "He is a living textbook of basketball."

"I call him 'Kodak,' " said Fitch when he was coaching the Celtics, "because his mind is constantly taking pictures of the whole court."

As for the matter of racism . . . while it was an issue that came to light under unpleasant circumstances, it was an unavoidable issue nonetheless. Before Isiah or his Detroit Piston teammate Dennis Rodman ever talked out of turn, after the 1987 Eastern Conference finals Bird was an issue because he was white and he was so good. The important thing to remember is that nobody ever talked about him being so white until long after they talked about him being so good.

In 1986, Portland's Michael Thompson was very direct about the matter. "He is the greatest white player to play a black man's sport." Cedric Maxwell agreed wholeheartedly. "Larry's a great player who's white. He's made us a great team, and he's responsible for a lot of fans coming to our games."

But as everyone eventually realized about Bird was that he wasn't a great white hope, but a guy who gave hope to those who were 6′ 9″, not particularly fast, not particularly athletic, and wanted to play basketball. Isiah said he was misunderstood because he only meant it humorously and not as a defamation. As Thomas eventually explained, "What I was referring to was not so much Larry Bird, but the perpetuation of stereotypes about blacks. When Bird makes a great play, it's due [according to commentators] to his thinking, and his work habits. It's all planned out by him. It's not the case for blacks. All we do is run and jump."

With Bird, it seemed most people were always talking about what made him so good. After all the obvious stuff—like his desire and his hustle and his second efforts—was covered, there was a chance to probe with a little more depth. those who *fooled* Larry, like his teammates and his coaches, knew what made him special. Leave it to Fitch to get technical on the subject of the Bird.

"Larry can create off a set play," the former Celtic coach explained, "and in the context of that play he can invent something that's never been done." In other words, Fitch was talking about moments when Bird would unexpectedly flip the ball over his shoulder to a teammate open under the basket.

That is probably the least-publicized perspective of Bird. What it is like to be on the other end of one of those no-look passes, or to be able to know if the game is on the line, that your team will win because you had Larry Bird. For that matter, what was it like to ride the team bus with Bird or walk through hotel lobbies while everybody was watching?

The view trailing the play is courtesy of Carl Nicks, who was the Indiana State guard in 1979 responsible for getting the ball to Bird, though Nicks wasn't always sure how it would come back. "Larry is the type of player who, if you take your eye off him just one second, you might get your nose busted with those passes he throws. You never know when he might just throw one off his head."

Rick Carlisle had the best point of view of Bird's ability. For several years, Carlisle was a Celtic reserve who watched Bird night after night from the team bench. "He had supreme confidence in his game. That's why he could always bury the game winner at the end. He thought everything he put up was going in."

But as the years went by, Bird became a good friend and a good teammate, one Carlisle liked to talk about. Bird had a knack for keeping things in perspective for the team. Apparently, the Bird Man made the rest of the Celtics realize why life in the NBA was so special.

"I can still see Larry getting on the bus after a shoot-around," Carlisle recalled. "He would say something like, 'Well, we just got done shooting basketball. Now it's time to go to our free hotel, have a free meal, then play the game. It's a tough life.' To Larry, it was special. He loved it. He couldn't imagine doing anything else."

Sometimes, though, Bird could leave other players speechless. Bobby Jones played against Bird more times than he wants to recount as a member of the Philadelphia 76ers in the 1980s. Jones was the best defensive forward in the game, the guy assigned to shadow Bird much of the time in those great Celtics-Sixers wars. More often than not, he came off the bench to do his duty, but in 1981 he had Bird all the way through a 34-point, 16-rebound performance.

"I think . . . I was . . . whew . . . how many points did he get? He's the best flat-footed faker I've ever seen," Jones said.

No opposing coach or player ever admitted to knowing how to stop Bird. Ramsay once said, "The best way I can think of is to keep the ball out of his hands. We try to keep him from handling the ball. If he touches it sixty times in an average game, we want to hold him to fifty. That way we can minimize the his opportunities to impact the game."

In the 1981 NBA championship series, Del Harris figured he could find a way to stop Bird. Put 6' 7" Robert Reid on him and watch Reid shadow Bird everywhere. If another player was going uncontested to the hole, Harris still wanted Reid not to leave Bird. That was the night of game 4 in Houston when Bird led all scorers with 27 points in a 102 91 victory.

Michael Cooper of the Lakers generally was accorded to be the one man who could hold Bird, though Milwaukee's Paul Pressey was always underrated in his ability to stay with the Bird as well. Still, Cooper's game plan wasn't anything extraordinary. "I tried to keep the ball out of his hands because he was such a creative player with the ball," said Cooper, the NBA's defensive Player of the Year in 1987. "But then if he would get it, I'd try to push him as far out as I can on the floor. But he hit forty-nine percent from out there, which is better than most people did from a lot closer. He scored thirty-three on me one night, but I still think I did a good job on him because he had to work for it."

There was one thing, however, they didn't know about Bird that M.L. Carr knew. "We saw it happen with Robert Reid and then with Michael Cooper. They say they're Birdbusters but they don't understand how much Larry Bird likes a challenge."

Those who understood what made Larry Bird great came right out and said so. In the search for superlatives to describe Bird, even the most educated speakers had trouble finding the right words. There was nobody in the game to compare to Larry. So they went to another game to look for the most dominating player they could find to accurately make comparisons. In hockey, Wayne Gretzky was named the National Hockey League's Most Valuable Player 7 times in a row. In the March 18, 1985 issue of *Time*, Tom Callahan realized Bird could only be compared to Gretzky because "they play a game with which we are not familiar."

There was more than one way of saying Bird was great.

"He is the consummate player, the best in the game," Julius Erving told *The New York Times* on February 10, 1985, just prior to the NBA All-Star Game. "He sleeps and drinks basketball. He's willing to pay the price to be great, something a lot of players don't want to do."

Everybody talked about this aspect of Bird as if they were saying something new and different. It didn't matter if it was a teammate, a coach, or the man who signed his paycheck. Everyone was biased when it came to Bird.

"He puts so much pressure on a team because he does so many things well," said former Chicago Bulls coach Jerry Sloan in 1981. "I don't think there's ever been a better player in the league."

"If I say Larry Bird is the best player," said Tiny Archibald, the man who made the Celtics go in the early 1980s, "then people say, 'He's on your team, that's why you're saying that.' I still say he's the best all-around player. He did more things for us than any other player did for his team."

Finally, some of the experts dropped the "all-around" and just called Bird the best.

"I used to vacillate," said Bob Cousy, the backcourt wizard on the great Celtic teams of the 1950s and early 60s. "The question of who was the greatest didn't seem relevant. But Bird came along with all the skills, all the things a basketball player has to do. I think he's the greatest."

Don Nelson, former Celtic, former Milwaukee Bucks coach, and full-time expert, was never one to mince words: "He's the best player ever to play the game."

John Wooden, who was the greatest college coach in the game when he was at UCLA, and a man whose basketball roots go back to Indiana State just like Bird, said, "I've always considered Oscar Robertson to be the best player in the game. Now I'm not so sure Larry Bird isn't." Added the Lakers' general manager Jerry West: "He is as nearly perfect as you can get in almost every phase of basketball."

"The one thing you have to avoid when you talk about Bird is statistics," Red Auerbach claimed. "It's his presence, the total game. He's the best passing forward I've ever seen. He's better than Bill Bradley, better than John Havlicek, better than all of them. He's like a Bob Cousy upfront and Cousy was without question the greatest passer who played the game until Bird. He will go down as one of the greatest of all time, if not the greatest.''

Larry Bird never liked to listen to that stuff, though. He always felt that the moment he started talking about himself would be the moment he stopped pushing himself. In other words, if he ever stopped to consider if he was truly the greatest player in the game, well, it was time to hang it up.

10

The King and His Court

LARRY BIRD WALKED OUT OF THE SHOWER AND, LIKE LOYAL subjects, a horde of reporters stood at attention as he passed. They lined the sides of his path as if to escort him to his throne, which doubled as the wooden stool in front of his dressing cubicle in the Boston Celtics' locker room. During the 1985–86 season such a coronation accompanied Bird wherever he played, for these were the people who went around paying homage to Larry as the king of the court. The media set out to spread the word that despite a nagging backache, a pain in his elbow, and a slow start, Larry Bird, the NBA's MVP of the past two seasons, was alive and swell. By midseason any ideas of Bird being dethroned were solemnly, if not spectacularly, laid to rest. The king was back and he was better than ever. Long live the king.

Bird had been considered part of the league's royalty ever since he came into the NBA, but in 1986 he would

reign supreme by winning his third consecutive Most
Valuable Player award. That feat put him in the com-
pany of 2 of the game's greatest conquering heroes.
Wild Chamberlain and Bill Russell had won 3 straight
MVPs, but no one else ever had. Not Magic. Not even
Kareem.

Magic had another truly magical season, all the more
spectacular because he led the league in assists for the
fourth straight year while spending the entire season
playing on a weak knee. But 1985–86 was a time to
honor Bird, who finished in the Top 10 of 5 major
statistical categories and was so good that mere numbers couldn't provide a sufficient tribute. Remember:
With Bird, you have to avoid statistics. For Larry, the
season was a culmination of everything that had enabled
him to climb to the top and be king of the hill. The
Celtics went to him more than ever as he exhibited his
passion for winning like never before. He worked so
hard that he realized during a sizzling stretch in February that "no one can guard me if I'm playing my
hardest." The league's best Birdbusters came out in
force, and in the end they all bowed down in respect to
his grace.

Even Celtics coach K.C. Jones was left in amaze-
ment. "You sit and wonder if what you see him doing
is really happening. And it really is."

Bird was playing his game like he had never done
before. He had developed his left hand so proficiently
that the people who played the numbers game recorded
stretches when Bird would hit 14 of his last 21 shots
with his left. He would bring the ball up the court on
offense, looking to be double-teamed just so he could
use a flurry of fakes to make the defense look pathetic.

There was a noticeable change in his attitude toward the game that season.

"I think Larry gets bored out there sometimes," said Celtic teammate Danny Ainge as the 1986 season headed into the home stretch. "I notice that he passes up these incredibly easy shots, and you can sense him thinking, 'Well, why don't I drive down the lane, get a few guys on me, and see what happens?'" Added Bird: "It happens. I do get bored. Then I look for a way to make it interesting."

Going into the season Bird made it clear that now that he was on top of the mountain it wasn't going to be easy to knock him off. In the NBA, being named MVP is tantamount to being the kingpin in the league, so Bird went on to prove he was the king of his court. By the time he wrapped up his third MVP trophy, Bird was also named the Player of the Year by *Sporting News*, which asked the NBA players themselves to vote on that award. He proved himself as the king of the 3-point shot by becoming the league's all-time leader in that category and by winning the NBA's long-distance shootout during All-Star weekend. He even led the league in free-throw shooting. He had 11 triple doubles during the season, the last of which came in the final game of the playoffs. That made Bird the playoff MVP for the second time in his career and, most importantly, it enabled Bird to end this glorious season with the only crowning achievement he ever cared about: the NBA championship.

When training camp for the 1985–86 season began, Bird had walked in as usual—3 hours early—to work on his shooting. McHale arrived early one day as well, and when he saw Bird moving up and down the court he wondered how everything was going. Bird said everything was fine. The worrying, you see, was left to the Celtic management. They knew Bird had struggled through the 1985 NBA finals with bursitis in the elbow of his primary shooting arm. Can you imagine how Auerbach and Jones would have felt had they known that Bird had injured his back while shoveling gravel during the summer? Even in the kingdom of French Lick, Bird was never above a little work.

Consequently, the first month of the season was not a particularly memorable one for Bird. He was scoring at more than 20 points a game from the opening tipoff of the campaign, but Larry could have done that left-handed by now. What was news was how he turned the ball over 7 times in the first half of a game against the New York Knicks on November 8. By the end of that month, Bird was thirteenth in the league in scoring, and when he hit for 47 points in a 132–124 defeat of Detroit on December 1, the Bird Man seemed to have found a cure for what had ailed him.

"My back was so bad in the pre-season that, really, I almost counted out the whole year," Bird said. "I could only shoot around for an hour or so, instead of my normal three or four hours, and I couldn't run any wind sprints so I got out of shape. Lately, the last month or so, I can feel myself getting back in shape, getting stronger, and it's made a difference."

This was proof that behind every successful king there was a good doctor. Bird had said he was in so much pain that he couldn't bend over or extend himself in any way. The difference in his game was noticeable. He was no longer knocking over the press table diving for loose balls, or stepping in anybody's Diet Coke while trying to extend some extra effort. The lack of effort came to light when the Celtics blew a 25-point third-quarter lead against the Knicks on Christmas Day—on national television—and lost in double overtime. It was the team's fourth loss in a row, and the first time the Celtics had lost 4 in a row since Bird came to Boston. Afterward, Bird went to see Dan Dyrek, a physical therapist who devised a special regimen for Bird to regain his health. It had almost been impossible to notice that Bird was playing in pain because the Celtics started the season by winning 11 of their first 13 games.

But all eyes were on Boston. The Lakers were breezing through the Western Conference en route to an 18–2 start, the best in team history. Magic was leading the league in assists midway through December with a 13.3 average, and it was so routine for the defending NBA champions that it was almost natural to overlook them. But then, this was the reason when everyone was playing for second.

First and foremost, Bird started playing like he was feeling no pain. And there was no better painkiller in the NBA than going out and playing your game like it was when it was great, really great. Larry was hooping up a storm by the new year, and his 41 points on January 12 helped bring Boston back from a 27-point first-half deficit to beat Atlanta, 125–122, in overtime. The Celtics swept through a 4–0 week by defeating Philadelphia 132–124, the team's seventh win in a row, and Bird led the way with 47 points.

What better way for Bird to see if he was back on track than by playing the Lakers? Within a month, the teams were scheduled to meet twice, their only seasonal bouts, once in each town. Everyone looked on the course of events as a preview to what might happen in the playoffs. Bird and Magic also used the games as a personal measuring stick.

The Celtics beat the Lakers in the Garden, 110–95, and in the Forum, 100–95. Boston beat L.A. out on the break and in the half-court game. Bird had 21 points and 12 rebounds in the first game and 22 points and 18 rebounds in the second, while Magic was left on the bench with his knee wrapped in ice. Earvin was too busy waging the battle of wounded knee, and he missed most of this part of the season due to this injury. He managed to play in the All-Star Game and the 2 games with the Celtics. He knew what they meant.

"We're keeping an eye on them just like they're keeping an eye on us," said Magic. "Right now, there's no doubt that Boston is a much better team."

Bird was, painfully, Bird. He dazzled in the second quarter by stealing a no-look pass by the Magic Man. Then Bird drove the baseline on offense and without looking threw a pass around Kareem to Paris for a lay-up. In the third quarter, he buried a bevy of jump shots: a 3-pointer, then a 20-foot J, then another 20-footer, and finally a high-arc'ing baseline swish. Afterward McHale said, "It should be a rule that everybody gets to play with Larry Bird for a week."

In the second game, Magic was a bit more healthy, which seemed to bring out a little something extra in Bird. He had 18 rebounds, twice as many as Kareem and 11 more than Lakers forward James Worthy. He scored a quiet 22 points, but he made his plays of the game on defense. With 4:26 left in the game, Worthy had just scored his thirty-fifth point to cut the Boston lead to 100–94. At the 3:51 mark, the Celtics called a timeout and put the game in Bird's hands by way of asking him to guard Worthy. Larry checked his foe into submission. Worthy scored just 2 more points the rest of the way, and it was home, James. Bob Cousy had said that the thing that makes a Celtic is his disdain for the opponent. Disdain was a pretty good way to describe Bird's feeling for losing at this point. "The team's personality comes from Larry Bird," said Bill Walton, the newest Celtic that season. "Never doubt that."

Between the Laker triumphs, Bird showed that long distance was the next best thing to being under the basket when he hit 3 decisive 3-point shots in a 105–103 win over the Sixers. Bird culminated a 13-game run with a 26.2 points-per-game average and .530 shooting from the field. Call it a run at the MVP award. Bird tried to downplay such an occurrence by saying he thought the Chicago Bulls' Michael Jordan, the league's newest sensation, should have won it last year. But Jordan was out with a broken foot, and even Bird was having trouble convincing himself not to at least think about what winning the MVP meant.

"You win that award," he began, "and you can say for one year you are the best in the world."

Everyone was playing to be second best. This was the NBA's long-distance shootout, of course, when Larry Bird was looking to add another jewel to his crown. This long-distance shooting competition pitted the NBA's best gunners against each other to see who could make the most shots out of 25 attempts from beyond the 3-point line. In 1986, the long-distance shootout was contrived along with the slam-dunk contest and the old-timers' game to spice up the NBA All-Star weekend.

Bird liked the idea because it gave him a chance to prove what he did best. And to Bird, the only thing he liked better than being the best was winning. While the league's best leapers were trashing the rim in the slam-dunk contest, Bird was getting ready to strut his stuff. Apparently, he thought the 24-footer was his best shot. "I'm like a gymnast," Bird said. "I'm into degree of difficulty."

He struggled through the preliminary competition, and when he made it to the final, he looked at his competitor, Craig Hodges of the Milwaukee Bucks, and said to him, "Now I know who is second." Bird missed his first shot, then hit 10 in a row. He finished with 18 of 25, good for the $10,000 first-place prize money. But money wasn't the point.

"I'm the king of three-point shooting," Bird exclaimed. "I always thought it, and now I have proven it. I've been pumped up for this for about a month. It was like a dare, because my teammates said I didn't have a chance."

Otherwise, All-Star weekend was nothing more extraordinary then it had been in previous seasons. Magic started the action by showing everyone else how to pass the basketball. He finished with 15 assists in limited action because of his ailing knee. Bird had 23 points, 8 rebounds, 5 assists, and 7 steals. With his East team trailing 53–46 midway through the second quarter, Bird scored 8 straight points, 6 on 3-point shots. With Bird and Isiah leading the way, the East used an 18–6 fourth-quarter run to pull out a 139–132 victory. The balloting for the game's MVP came down to Bird,

Magic, and Isiah. This was the only MVP this season Bird did not win. And it was the only MVP Magic could never win. "Oh, they let me win," Isiah mused afterward.

Midway through the season the Celtics were rolling with a 13-game winning streak as Bird continued to stay in the Top 10 of 5 major statistical categories. He was fifth in scoring at 25 points a game; ninth in rebounds at 9.5; seventh in 3-point shooting; seventh in steals with a 2.29 average; and he was leading the league in free throws at a .905 clip.

And Larry Bird was only warming up.

During a 6-game stretch the last 2 weeks of February he set out to prove how valuable he could be. On February 13 he burned Seattle for 31 points, 15 rebounds, and 11 assists, and the next night he was even better. Against Portland Bird had 14 rebounds, 11 assists, and 47 points. He hit a 3-pointer to tie the game with 6 seconds left, and then he hit a 10-foot jumper with 3 seconds left in overtime to give Boston a 120–119 victory. Only a second-quarter ejection kept him from making it a consecutive-games streak, for he had already scored 18 when he was kicked out of the game. He came back with 36 points, 12 rebounds, and 11 assists in a 115–100 defeat of Golden State, and then on February 23 he struck for 30 points, 11 rebounds, and 12 assists against Indiana. Two nights later it was 24 points, 18 rebounds, and 13 assists in a 91–74 win over the Knicks, and the streak climaxed with a 20-point, 13-rebound, and 12-assists performance in a 124–108 victory over the L.A. Clippers. Larry Bird was doing the triple double.

Bird, however, avoided statistics. Even if he did lead

the league in foul shooting it would net him an extra $30,000, according to an incentive clause in his contract, yet he said, "I have only one real goal in this league: to play every minute of every single game." Bird was averaging 38.9 minutes of 48 per game. Since the All-Star Game Bird was averaging 30.8 points, 13.1 rebounds, and 7.8 assists per game. Indiana Pacers coach George Irvine took one look at those numbers and said, "As an all-around player, there's never been anyone better."

Above and beyond everyone, Bird played the game with his head. In the technical aspect of the thinking man's game, Bird would plot out his offensive moves and use pump fakes, head fakes, and jab steps to outwit the opposing defense. He would take on the double-teams and leave a trail of dumbfounded defenders in his path to the basket. "After a while," said teammate Scott Wedman, "the man guarding Larry didn't know whether he was coming or going."

But Bird also knew how to play mind games with the competition. In a game against Detroit, Isiah Thomas had just left a Piston flurry to put his team out in front. During a break in the action, Bird walked up to Isiah and said, "Are you through?"

"No," Thomas charged back.

"Well, you're through now because it's my turn." Bird took control; the Celtics won 130–123.

Bird had also made himself the two-handed man. He fashioned an ability to lead with his right when he started shooting, then deliver the knockout punch with his left. "I remember a game," said David Greenwood when he was playing with the Chicago Bulls, "when he

kept yelling, 'Left hand, left hand.' And he hit everything, including a left-hander while going out of bounds.''

He had turned rebound from a science into an art
form. To Bird, this was a simple matter. ''Most rebounds are taken below the rim. That's where I get
mine.''

And, believe it or not, his passing was even better. In
one moment when he may have been looking to do
something to make it interesting, Bird was triple-teamed
in the corner when he threw the ball right between Joe
Barry Caroll's legs into the waiting hands of Walton.
''I'm not sure how I did that one myself,'' Bird said.

When *Sports Illustrated* featured Bird on his fourth
cover shot in 1986, the title to the story read, ''As
Nearly Perfect As You Can Get.'' In the 2 weeks after
such an issue was raised, Bird averaged 37 points, 10
rebounds, and 6 assists over 6 games while shooting
65% from the field. He also hit 19 of 26 shots from
3-point range. He had 50 points in a win over Dallas on
March 10, and he came back with 43 points 2 nights
later in a win over Cleveland. He *was* as nearly perfect
as you can get.

What more could he accomplish during the regular
season? The Celtics were on their way to a 40–1 record
in the Garden, including an NBA record of 29 in a row,
and 67–15 for the season, which was the best mark ever
in the Bird era. On March 23, he hit 5 of 6 from 3-point
range to become the all-time league leader in that category, and he finished that 129–96 win at Houston with
43 points in 24 minutes. But, then, leave it to the Magic
Man to let Bird know what was left to conquer this
year.

''The only way the ego gets fed is when you put a

diamond [championship ring] on your finger. Then you can go out on the street and feel good.''

The Celtics finished the regular season as the fourth-winningest team in NBA history. Bird finished fourth in scoring at 25.8 points per game and seventh in rebounding with 9.8 a game. He was fourth in 3-point shooting, and he was the only non-guard to finish among the Top 10 in steals with 2.02 a game. On the final day of the season, Bird went 7-for-7 from the foul line to beat out Golden State's Chris Mullin for the free-throw shooting title. Bird finished with an .8963 percentage to Mullin's .8957. That was worth $30,000—but, then, it wasn't the money.

When it came to the playoffs, though, Bird was money in the bank. His array of bank shots, baseline drives, and bounce passes enabled the Celtics to sweep the Chicago Bulls in the first round of the playoffs. Jordan came back from his foot injury and in the first 2 games scored 49 and 63 points, the latter being an NBA record. But he wasn't the Most Valuable Player in this series.

Bird had his sights set on the top of the mountain, and on the way to the top he hoped to climb right over Magic and the Lakers. Earvin was on his way up as well, having dished out a record 48 assists in a 3-game sweep of San Antonio in the first round of the playoffs. When the Celtics took the Eastern Conference semifinal series from Atlanta in 5 games, Bird finished off the Hawks with 36 points and 10 rebounds in a 132–99 final victory. But what he was most proud of on this night was that the team held Atlanta to just 6 points in all 12 minutes of the third quarter.

In the Eastern finals, the Celtics sent the Milwaukee

Bucks packing just as quickly. What Milwaukee coach Don Nelson did on his summer vacation that year was wonder about the final game of the series. Bird scored 30 points, 14 of the team's last 17 in the final 4:06 of a 110–98 victory. For Bird this was another step up. In the fourth quarter he spotted up at the 3-point line and hit 4 straight shots, the last just before the final buzzer.

"Not only did he break their hearts," said McHale, "but he created a monster. In thirty-five years they'll be talking about that game when Bird stood out at the 3-point line and put 'em in. Every year the shots will go out three or four feet farther. He was unbelievable. It was like taking a twenty-two and shooting balloons."

The Lakers didn't have it so easy. After disposing of the Dallas Mavericks, 4 games to 1 in the Western Conference semifinals, L.A. had to take on Houston for the Western championship 40 hours later. Los Angeles took the first game, 119–107, with Magic right on top of his game. But with 26 points and 18 assists, little did he know that it would be the team's last win of the season. Houston won the series, 4–1, when Ralph Sampson hit a game-winning shot at the final buzzer of game 5. The Rockets had kept the Lakers from being the first NBA team since the 1969 Celtics to win back-to-back titles, and in the process set up the 1986 Celtics to become one of the greatest teams of all time.

If Boston had swept Houston in 4 games, it would have made them 82–18 for the year, by far the best ever. And in one move of game 2 of the NBA finals Bird again proved he was the best ever. He had dribbled into the corner and trapped himself into as double-team a step inside the 3-point line. Houston's mammoth 7' center, Akeem Olajuwon, came over to help out on defense. Bird held the ball above his head and started his arms forward as if to pass. Akeem backed off. Bird pulled the ball back and dropped an easy 3-pointer. Bird finished the team's second victory of the series with 31 points, 8 rebounds, and 7 assists. Said Olajuwon: "He's the greatest player I've ever seen." Welcome to the club, Akeem.

Just prior to game 3, the NBA announced Bird had won his third consecutive MVP. The voting wasn't even close. Dominique Wilkins was second and Magic was third. Said Bird: "I don't feel my career is over yet, and I feel I can win it a lot more times. I've been striving to be the best, and once you're considered the best, you don't want to get knocked off. Once I got my first MVP, there was a burning desire to get another one. To win an award that proves you're the best is important because I know how hard I work."

Then it was enough with being king for a day. Game 3 of the finals was set for the tipoff, and for Bird that meant it was back to work. Even in defeat, a 106–104 loss, Bird was spectacular with a triple double: 25 points, 15 rebounds, and 11 assists. And Larry was still saving his best for last.

Olajuwon had hurt Boston badly with 40 points in the victory. In game 4, Jones assigned Bird to drop off his man and double-team Akeem when he had the ball. Olajuwon finished game 4, a 106–103 Celtics win, with 20 points and plenty of frustration. Bird had 21 points, 10 rebounds, and 9 assists, and so an off-night (17 points) in a game 5 loss was to be expected even for the Bird. He was, at least, part human.

In the playoffs, Bird was averaging 25.5 points, 9.5 rebounds, and 8 assists per game. He was shooting

54.5% from the field and 95.2% from the foul line. After 82 games of the regular season his numbers were up. That alone was enough to make him the MVP. But for those who weren't keeping an eye on the stat sheet, in this season Bird ran his streak of consecutive games scoring in double figures to 205, and he played in all 82 games for the third time in his 7-year career. And he was still saving the best for last.

In the sixth game of the 1986 NBA finals, Bird had 29 points, 11 rebounds, and 12 assists in a 114–97 victory, which brought the Celtics their sixteenth world championship. Bird was named the MVP of the playoffs. With his team leading 84–61, he picked up a loose ball at half-court and instead of driving to the bucket he spotted up at the 3-point line and dropped one final jumper from long distance.

"Everything I took was on target tonight," Bird said. By the time it was all over, the fans in the Garden were ready to go crazy. But before the members of this capacity crowd stood up and cheered, they bowed down and paid their respects to Larry Bird. They knew who was king of this court.

INSTANT REPLAY
Sixth Sense

THE BIRD MAN FELT THE MAGIC IN HIM THIS SUNDAY morning, the day of the sixth game of the 1986 NBA championship series. The Houston Rockets were about to become nothing more than mere data with which to document one of Larry's most amazing qualities. What happened made the Rockets realize Bird was extraordinary, and afterward they were wondering if maybe he was extra-terrestrial.

As Larry took this game, which would wrap up the Boston Celtics' sixteenth NBA championship, into his own hands, he was showing off his sixth sense. Some source from within enabled Larry to run faster, jump higher, and shoot better when he could smell and taste how sweet the victory would be.

"My intensity was as high for this game as any game," he said afterward. It was as if on the sixth game God created Larry Bird, then he rested and joined everybody else who was watching the Bird soar on this Sunday.

Bird made Houston think there were 3 of him out there with 29 points, 11 rebounds, and 12 assists. The *Sporting News* sensed Bird had something else, with his out-of-this-world play. In March of 1986, that publication unveiled its "All Crunch-Time Team," and Bird was the most valuable player on the squad including, among others, Isiah and Kareem. (Magic was on the second team.) "Crunch Time" was any time the game was on the line and it came down to one player to win or lose. Bird was the ultimate winner in this situation for a very good reason.

"Hey, it's a gutsy move to take that last shot which can win the game," he said. "I've seen guys who don't want to shoot at all in the last five minutes of a game, let alone the last five seconds. I don't want them on my team."

Bird hesitantly questioned his company after the Celtics lost game 5 of the series. He took just 13 shots in the game and scored but 17 points. What was so unusual, however, was that Bird went long stretches of the game without touching the ball. As the Celtics left Houston after the loss, Bird looked at his team and said, "Give me the ball in game six and we'll win."

So when a ball squirted loose in the first quarter of the game, Bird dove for the rock with reckless abandon. He recovered the fumble, but no teammate was around to hand off to. He screamed to Ainge, "Come to the ball." Moments later, Bird spotted McHale streaking downcourt and threw the long pass. McHale didn't see Bird or the ball. "Look up, damn it," the Bird Man muttered. "When Larry talks, we all listen," said Boston assistant coach Jimmy Rodgers. Added McHale, "It's embarrassing not to play the way Larry wants you to play when he's playing that way."

Bird was intent on doing everything in his power to win the game, and that was his sixth sense. He wanted to take the rest of the team along for the ride. "You see those five fingerprints on the back of his jersey," K.C. Jones said after the game. "That's because Larry carried us all the way, and I grabbed hold at the hotel."

On the second play of the game, Bird swiped the ball so surprisingly from Rodney McCray that Rodney was left dead in his tracks. Bird made 2 more steals in the first quarter, both when Akeem Olajuwon tried to back in on the Celtic defense in the low post. Bird left his defensive assignment to double-team Akeem and swatted the ball from behind when the big man tried to go up with a shot. Bird scored just 7 points in the opening period, but 2 came when he took an offensive rebound away from Olajuwon and McCray and put it back up for the bucket. Was that his sixth sense taking over, or was that just Bird?

Bird controlled the boards with 8 rebounds in the first half when his scoring wasn't much of a factor. When Boston went on the offensive, Bird took the ball on the side of the floor his teammates cleared out for him. He backed in on McCray as if to toy with the young forward. McHale, Parish, and Walton alternated cutting through the lane to get a pass from Bird right in stride to the hole.

When Houston finally figured out that maybe another defender should be accorded to Bird, Larry took the double-team to the base line, and whipped the ball to Ainge or Dennis Johnson who were open for short jump shots. Most of Bird's 12 assists came during a second-quarter run which put the Celtics up 54–38 at the half. Did Bird make it look easy? "Yeah, I would say it looked easy," he said afterward.

As Bird played 46 of the 48 minutes, he never stopped diving for loose balls, pushing the Celtics upcourt on the fast break and doing everything in his power to make sure the Celtics put the crunch on the Rockets early in the second half. His first quarter with 7 points, 4 assists, 4 rebounds, and 3 steals apparently was merely a preview. Bird turned the third quarter into crush time. He worked a give-and-go with Parish for a lay-up, then buried a 3-point shot to put the team up by 20 points. A behind-the-back bounce pass to Walton was good for another hoop, and then he saved his best for last. With time running out on the 24-second clock, Bird tried a spin move to the hole. His path was blocked. So he took the ball out to the 3-point stripe and launched a jumper right before the 24-second clock expired. The Rockets' hopes of an NBA title expired shortly thereafter.

Afterward, Walton discussed Bird's exploits with some members of the media, who suggested his 29 points was not all that exceptional considering he averaged 26 during the regular season. "With all that pressure out there and with everything else he did, twenty-nine points was exceptional," Walton confirmed. "We still haven't seen the best of Larry Bird because we aren't good enough to push him as hard as he can be pushed."

11

Laying Down the Law

LET'S SAY ARNOLD BECKER IS REPRESENTING MR. EARVIN Johnson Jr., who has come before the court to demand equal time. If nothing else, this hearing should serve to set the record straight about who is the best in the game. You know, as in "Magic and the Bird are the best in the game." It seems that some time around May or June of 1986, the state of California hit Magic with a gross miscarriage of justice, when all judgments returned ruled that this Larry Bird was without a doubt the game's greatest player. Sure, there was plenty of testimony to support such a verdict, but recent findings indicated that during the period of November of 1986 through June of 1988, Earvin "Magic" Johnson took the law, along with the game, into his own hands. He remained the most unselfish player in the game by way of leading the NBA in assists for a fourth and fifth time. And he also became the leading scorer on what was arguably the best team in the history of the game. This time, the Los Angeles Lakers won back-to-back NBA championships in 1987 and 1988 due to Magic Johnson, not just with him. This was *his* Lakers team, the first to repeat as champions since the 1968–69 Boston Celtics. He even won the award for being the league's Most Valuable Player in 1987, which we feel should reestablish his right and his privilege to be considered right up there with Bird as the best in the game, ever. Anything else would be unconstitutional.

To be fair to Mr. Bird, he probably had his best season ever in 1987–88—better than his MVP years—but that only attests to the prowess of Mr. Johnson. Bird's ability to stay on top of his game only serves to prove how hot Magic was just to stay up there in the league. The evidence is overwhelming.

Furthermore, Magic wasn't even 100% mentally or physically when the 1986–1987 season began. His sister Mary was fighting an ongoing battle with lung disease, and her prognosis was not good. Once more, all the years of fast-breaking had taken a toll on Earvin. His knees were aching all the time, and he developed tendonitis in his left Achilles tendon so badly that he was forced to sit out of practice periodically.

In his 7 years before the 1986–87 season, Johnson had career averages of 17.5 points and nearly 10 assists per game, numbers that were only spectacular enough to make him the best point guard in the game. During the summer of 1986, coach Pat Riley sent a letter to magic about his prospects for the upcoming season. Riley challenged Johnson to make the Lakers *his* team. Kareem would still be the big guy, but the coach asked Magic to pick up his scoring to a 20-plus clip while still being the set-up man for the team's fearless fast break. In basketballese, Riley was asking Magic to raise his game. It was a step on the way to the top of the mountain.

Earvin came through with a career-best 23.9 scoring average for the season and he still led the league in assists with a 12.2 mark. The Lakers finished the season with a 65–17 and the NBA championship, and they breezed through the playoffs to beat the Celtics 4 games to 2 in the NBA finals. There was so much evidence to attest to Earvin's overall dominance that season.

"Earvin was just awesome," said the coach. "I knew he could do this, but he was making shots and drives that even surprised him. He's doing spin moves and dipping his shoulder and going through the defenses, doing basketball shots no one else can make."

The Lakers had opened the season with a loss to the Houston Rockets, while Bird had 38 points and 33 points in pair of Celtic victories over the Indiana Pacers and Washington. But, then, Bird was ejected in the first half of a game against Milwaukee; he missed some games after straining his Achilles tendon; and the Celtics' 48-game home-court winning streak came to an end on November 13 with a 117–109 loss to Washington. Within another month the tables had turned completely. On December 22, the Lakers came into the Garden and trashed the Celtics 117–110.

The proof that Magic was now soaring like a Bird came with his 31-point, 8-assist, 7-rebound effort in the victory. As Magic sat in the locker room afterward with his knees wrapped in ice packs—a familiar sight during the season—he said he was only 90% physically. Magic was leading the Lakers in scoring with a 21.3 average (and climbing), while taking a meager 16 shots a game, so it wasn't as if he were being a ball-hog.

More than his length-of-the-court, helter-skelter drives to the bucket, Magic was now scoring by posting up smaller guards down low and powering in for a lay-ups. He also was stepping back, and dropping a one-handed push shot from the perimeter. His knees may have felt old, but his mind made him feel like he was back on the playground. This was the youthful exuberance that he'd first brought to the Lakers in 1979 when they called him ''Buck''—as in ''Young Buck.''

He was bucking a trend. Magic had a score to settle. During a 3-game stretch in late December when Abdul-Jabbar was on the bench with eye problems, Magic took control. He scored 34 points in the process of whipping Dallas, and he had 38 the next night in a rout at Houston. He finished the flurry with a career-high 46 points in a victory over Sacremento. With Magic scoring more, so were the Lakers. They won their eighth straight over Denver, 147–109, then, after dropping a pair, came back with a 6-game run. The sixth victory was a culmination for Johnson, who had his third triple double of the season with 29 points, 11 assists, and 10 rebounds. L.A. was 34–10, the best record in the NBA.

Magic was becoming the people's choice. When All-Star ballots were returned for the 1987 game, he was the leading vote-getter in the Western Conference. His average was up to 24.3 to go with 12 assists per game. But for the first time he was accounting for more scoring with his shooting than with his passing, and his passing was still the best in the game. He had answered Riley's challenge: Was it too premature to think about the MVP? Could he be the first guard to win the award since Oscar Robertson had in 1964?

"I'd like to win the MVP, but it doesn't eat at me that I haven't won it. If I can't win it the way I play, fine. What can I say? But when you play for a certain number of years and accomplish things in your profession, you'd like to finally close the book and feel you didn't let anything get out."

Further testimony to the fact that the Lakers had become Magic's team was in the works. When he picked up the scoring load, he had become the main option in the team's offense. The main option in any offense is the one guy the team tries to set up in position to score. He is more often than not the big guy. With Kareem, Magic had always been the set-up man. In the scheme of things in the past there was one offensive set which featured him as the main man. In the 1987 season, the Lakers developed 7 or 8 ways to set up Earvin.

"Feels good to have someone get you the ball once in a while," Magic said.

The Lakers gave him the ball on February 19, when they pranced into the Boston Garden for the last regular season showdown with the Celtics. Afterward, they danced out as Magic scored 39 points, and added 10 assists and 7 rebounds. He even hit a 40-foot shot just before the end of third period to cut a one-time 17-point Boston lead to 81–77. The Lakers prevailed, 106–103, due largely to Magic's whirling lay-up on which he was fouled with 1:29 to play. The 3-point play put the Lakers up 98–97. He hit a drop-back, one-hand push shot off one leg to make 102–99, and that was the ballgame.

The Celtics provided their own testimony. "They're the best team in the league," said coach K.C. Jones.

"And Magic is the best player in the league right

now," added Danny Ainge, who spent most of this night one step behind Johnson. The roll continued with a 147–115 blowout of San Antonio in which Magic had 11 assists. That made him the ninth player in league history to accumulate more than 6,000 assists in his career.

But there was no cause for celebration. Mary had lost her bout with her lung problems. She died in January, and Magic never really said anything about it to anyone. Michael Cooper and Byron Scott provided some solace, but for the first time Earvin wanted to handle this thing alone. "You know you put it all on your shoulders, and sometimes you need an outlet," he said. "My outlet was playing games. But there was no talking outlet and that hurt. I just decided to dedicate this season to her and hope everything would work out."

So Magic went about his business. In the All-Star Game most of his 18 assists were to Seattle's Tom Chambers, who scored 37 points in the Western Conference's overtime victory. Chambers, however, was named the MVP—largely because the game was held in Seattle where he played for the Supersonics. This was the only MVP out of Magic's reach, but in the end Kareem knew his teammate had been responsible for the victory as much as anyone else. "Thanks," said the big fella as he left the locker room after the game. Kareem had already cast his vote for Magic as MVP.

Most observers were amazed that Magic could raise his scoring average to 24.3 yet still dish out 12 assists per game. As if this was some kind of phenomenon. As Kareem Abdul-Jabbar testified, Earvin's ability to accomplish that made the Lakers a better team. It made the Lakers *Magic's* team.

"We were too committed to one specific concept," the big man said. "We weren't utilizing all the potential we had. It's more of a team with Magic running the show. I think he should be the MVP. He's making the crucial contribution to a very fine team."

Cooper thought that all things considered, Magic was still more or less the same. "When he started to score, people thought it was something unnatural, but I've been with Magic eight years now, and I can feel the aura around him. He does what he has to do to win. When he starts wiggling his shoulders to the side, he makes everyone go. When you see that, it's a sign to start falling in line."

Things were falling into place for Magic's team. With a 128–111 victory over Detroit on March 25, L.A. wrapped up its sixth consecutive Pacific Division championship and the seventh in the 8 years Magic had been in town. In the first round of the playoffs, the team completely obliterated Denver. With an NBA-record 82-point first half in the first game, the Lakers never looked back. Sweeping Golden State in the Western Conference semifinals was even easier.

As the Western Conference finals against Seattle began, Earvin let loose again. He had 19 points, 11 assists, and 7 rebounds in a 92–87 win to start the series. All the while his defense never rested. A quick review of Magic's season to date was astounding. He finished the campaign with 997 assists, and he nearly became just the third player in NBA history to record more 1,000 assists in a single season. He topped the 40-point plateau 3 times after reaching that number twice in his previous seven seasons. He took 390 more shots from the field than ever before and 199 more foul shots, and he still came close to his career averages from the floor and the foul line. He had 11 triple doubles in the regular season, one more than Bird in his 1986 MVP season.

Finally, on May 18, all precincts reported. Magic Johnson was the only player in the league to be named on all 78 ballots cast by members of the media for the league's Most Valuable Player award. He received 65 first-place votes and finished with 733 points to beat out the Chicago Bulls' Michael Jordan by 284 points for the moment he had been waiting for. Bird was third in the race for the MVP with 271 points and one loyal first-place vote.

"This is more than I ever dreamed of," said Earvin, who was only the second guard in NBA history to win the award. "I think I'm still living the dream now. It's like a fairy tale. I don't know how to express my feelings.

"This award, it belongs to my father. I'm living for him, in a sense, playing in the NBA. I'm going to give this to him. I hope he'll be proud.

"I always thought I would never win it. I always felt I had to score more to have a chance to win it. I wanted to win it, yes, as long as it was in the team concept. I'd like to thank Larry Bird for having an off-year."

Even Bird, who averaged 28 points a game, 9 rebounds, and 7.8 assists, cast his vote for the Magic Man this year. "I've always said this and I haven't changed my opinion. Magic is the best player in the league. If I had to take a player, there's no question who I would take. Magic is head and shoulders above everybody else. He makes everybody around him better."

Proof of such a result came in game 3 of the Western finals. With 7:35 to play and the Lakers winning 101–98,

Magic checked back into the game despite having 5 fouls. He hit Cooper with a no-look pass for a lay-up, then set up James Worthy for a pair of alley-oop slam dunks off the lob. He drove for a lay-up, turned it into a 3-point play, and the Lakers led 112–104. The series ended 2 nights later.

Meanwhile, the Celtics were struggling in an attempt to reach the NBA finals for the fourth straight season. It took a miraculous steal by Bird to salvage victory in game 5, and he had to play his best to fend off the pesky Pistons in the seventh game of the Eastern Conference finals.

The steal may have been the single greatest play in Bird's career. It was a physically outstanding play, but the sequence of events was amazing. With 5 seconds left and the Pistons leading game 5, 107–106, Detroit had the ball out of bounds with Isiah Thomas set to inbound. Thomas lobbed a soft pass to Bill Laimbeer at center court. Bird, who'd ended the last play on his behind by the base line after having his last shot blocked, rushed into the big picture, took the ball from Laimbeer, and passed to Dennis Johnson, who hit a game-winning lay-up. He had 37 points, 9 rebounds, and 9 assists in a 117–114 final-game victory.

Bird even had 3 key offensive rebounds during a sequence in the final 3:06 which the Pistons are still trying to explain. Danny Ainge shot from 3-point range and missed. Bird grabbed the rebound and missed another 3-pointer. Parish got that rebound and missed a follow-up shot. Bird grabbed that rebound, passed to Johnson, who passed back to Ainge, who finally hit a 3-pointer. It gave the Celtics an insurmountable 102–99 lead, but the feeling was that perhaps Boston's and Bird's luck had run out.

So much for equal time. The Lakers came out running in the first game of the championship and never stopped. In a 126–113 victory, Magic triggered 35 fast breaks and scored 29 points. The only outside shooting he did in this game was in the form of pull-up jumpers off the fast break. The momentum continued through a 141–122 second-game blowout.

As the series shifted to the Boston Garden, the Lakers talked of sweeping the Celtics in 4 straight. Boston escaped game 3 with a 109–103 victory, but Magic had 32 points in the loss, and that was the scary part. The Celtics had an 11-point lead in the fourth game, but the Lakers defense helped to quickly erase that margin. L.A. trailed 106–105 with 14 seconds left when the Lakers called a timeout to set up the final play. Nothing fancy. Magic took the ball, dribbled across the lane, and swished a running junior sky hook, the smaller version of the kareem commodity. Boston took game 5, but that merely set up the grand finale.

In one exquisite quarter of run-and-gun basketball, Magic brought this season to its culmination (Or was it a coronation?) With a 30-point third quarter, the Lakers ran away with a 106–93 win to wrap up the championship in 6 games. Magic had 16 points, 19 assists, and 8 rebounds, but in the third quarter he had 12 points and 8 assists. He anchored the team's defense, which gave up just 12 points in the period. Magic was unanimously chosen the MVP of the playoffs.

"He played with enough intensity this season for the other four guys on the floor." said Kareem. Mychal Thompson was preparing to return to his native Bahamas for the summer, and he extended an invitation to Magic to come down for a visit. Magic accepted, and Thompson was ecstatic; Magic was well-beloved there.

"When he gets there," Thompson said, "they'll treat him like the king of kings. And right now, that's exactly what he is in the NBA."

Magic was so on top of the game that as soon as the 1987 season ended, Riley predicted that the Lakers would become the first team to win back-to-back titles since 1969. In the NBA, such an occurrence was almost above the law. But Riley and Magic and the Lakers were looking for a new ruling.

So the case wasn't closed; not yet anyway. It was indisputable that Bird came back in the best shape of his life after spending the entire summer pumping iron. In the past, he had been known as a wide body for his ability to take up space defensively with his massive frame. Now he was *hard* body. He finished the season with a 29.9 scoring average and second in the balloting for MVP to Michael Jordan, who led the league in scoring and became the first guard since Magic to win the award.

But it was not about MVP awards anymore. The game was about winning championships—back-to-back ones, to be exact—and Magic's motivation to such an accomplishment came from within. He started the season with 26 points in a 113–109 defeat of Seattle, and Magic had 10 points during a crucial fourth-quarter run. Bird was hot, and Boston didn't lose its first game of the season until November 22 when Bird went down with an ankle injury.

The game was about winning and losing, and when the Lakers came in to the Garden to meet the Celtics on December 17, Magic proved he was the ultimate winner. With the game tied at 113, Magic stole a pass from Bird, and set Kareem up for a sky hook which rimmed out. Ainge made 1 of 2 free throws with 4 seconds left to apparently seal the Lakers' fate. On the final play, Magic came off a pair of screens, took an in-bounds pass, and hit a one-handed push shot from just inside the 3-point line to win the game. It was a bank shot, no less. "You almost expect him to do something like that," said the Celtics' Jerry Sichting of Magic, who had 18 points, 17 rebounds, and 8 rebounds. Johnson added: "I live for these situations."

Apparently, Earvin was living right. In a 131–114 victory at Philadelphia on December 28, Magic had 26 points and 17 assists, and L.A. was sporting a 26–10 record, the best in the league. Magic posted up his sixth triple double of the season in 110–101 victory over Chicago, the Lakers fourteenth in a roll. By contrast, when Bird scored 39 points with 17 rebounds and 10 assists in a 136–120 win over San Antonio, it was his first triple double of the season. One week later, however, Bird broke his nose in a game against Denver.

And so it went that season. Despite more than few breakdowns, the Celtics still won the Atlantic Division title by 11 games. The only break that mattered to the Lakers was the fast break until the end of the season. Magic suffered a groin pull and missed 3 games, 2 of which the team lost. He missed some action down the stretch when the Lakers lost 5 of their last 8 regular-season contests. Would Magic's injuries be the team's Achilles heel?

Boston, however, still had one last hurrah. In the seventh game of the Eastern Conference semifinals, Bird let fly with one final flurry. Consider, however, the danger, because this was the first conference semifinal series the Celtics played that went more than 5 games since they'd lost to the Bucks in 1982. But the fourth quarter of game 7 against the Atlanta Hawks was a thing of beauty. Bird hit 9 of 10 shots in the quarter, scored 20 points in the final 12 minutes of the final period, and finished with 34 for the game. He and the Hawks' Dominique Wilkins turned the game into their personal one-on-one, with Bird winning 20–16. He scored on a variety of baseline jumpers, lean-in bank shots, and drives to the hoop. He hit from 3-point range, and he hit for a 3-point play. With 26 seconds left, he split the defense for a running, one-hand scoop shot to make it 114–109, and victory was all but assured.

"I've seen many of his great fourth quarters," said Celtics' assistant coach Jimmy Rodgers. "But I don't ever remember him ever having a fourth quarter like that. And you know it was absolutely necessary. Everything he did was so significant."

In the Eastern Conference finals against Detroit, Bird didn't have a single good quarter and neither did the Celtics. They shot 32% as a team, one point lower than what Bird shot from the field in the 6-game series. There was no way for Bird to steal this one as the Pistons won in 6 games.

"It was probably the worst shooting series I've ever had," Bird said. "It's too early to go home for the summer. You don't want to go home right now."

So much for a closing argument, but Bird has always said that what fans remember is what you did for them last. And the way Magic willed the Lakers to the 1988 NBA title was the final entry on this season's docket.

The Lakers endured consecutive 7-game series against Utah in the conference semifinals and Dallas in the Western finals to get to the championship series. Once there, the Pistons pushed the Lakers through 7 games. But despite aching knees and a throbbing Achilles, Earvin's legs never gave out from under him.

Detroit won the first game, 105–93, in Los Angeles, but Earvin still had 28 points and 10 assists. And he was playing with the flu. He didn't even practice before the second game, and he came back with 23 points, 7 rebounds, and 11 assists in a 108–96 victory.

That meant some home cooking for Magic by way of traveling to Detroit for the next 3 games of the series. Since Lansing was but 50 miles from Detroit, Earvin Sr. could sit there and watch his son play in person for the first time in an NBA final. A 99–86 win for the Lakers put them ahead 2–1 and one step closer to the big cake. The reward for such an effort was a big piece of sweet potato pie and the rest of the feast Christine Johnson had cooked up for the team after the victory. It was hard to tell which was sweeter: Magic's 18 points on 7-for-8 shooting, 14 assists, and 6 rebounds—or the pie.

Magic was in full stride. In game 3, he came down court, dribbled twice between his legs, and canned a running hook shot. On the next break, the defense backed off, so he swished an 18-foot jumper. The next time down, he was surrounded. But A.C. Green was open under the hoop. Magic looked one way, then hurled the ball the other to Green. That was the no-look pass at its best because all the Pistons were caught looking the other way.

That the Pistons went ahead 3 games to 2, and that the Lakers had to win the sixth game 103–102 on 2 dramatic free throws by Kareem in the closing seconds, only set the tempo for the seventh-game showdown. It couldn't have been better for Magic. He was playing against his best friend Isiah Thomas, and the 2 even tried to fool everyone into thinking this was a war by almost getting into a fight in game 5. Later, they kissed and made up, and they kissed before every game just for good measure. All's fair in love and basketball.

Thomas had scored 43 points in game 6, but he sprained his ankle so badly that he was on crutches the morning of game 7. He played 28 minutes in the contest, but that was not nearly enough. And so with another immaculate quarter of fast-break basketball, the Lakers put the Pistons away. L.A. ran out to a 15-point lead in the third quarter and held on for a 108–105 triumph.

The win gave the Lakers their fifth NBA title in the 1980s. It made them comparable to other great dynasties in sports—like the Packers of the 60s, the Yankees of the 20s, the Steelers of the 70s, and, yes, even the Celtics of the 1960s, the last team to win back-to-back NBA championships.

"There's no question this is the best team I've ever played on," said the Magic Man. "It's fast, it can shoot and rebound, it has inside people, it has everything. I've never played on a team that had everything."

More than anything else, the team had Magic.

Case closed.

INSTANT REPLAY

Gimme A Break

EVEN IN SLOW MOTION MAGIC JOHNSON SEEMED TO BE moving at top speed. He galloped up the middle of the court, turning his head from side to side, and even cracked a little smile as if to pose for the television camera zooming in on his every step. Magic looked to James Worthy filling the lane to his right and then to A.C. Green coming up fast on his left. As if the ball were on a yo-yo, he faked left and dished right to Worthy for the slam dunk. This was the stuff of which highlight films are made.

This was also a picture-perfect fast break in the third quarter of the seventh game of the 1988 NBA finals against Detroit. For this one quarter the Lakers ran the fast break with reel-to-reel perfection. For one momentous 12-minute period, Magic was high-stepping and pump-faking and throwing those no-look passes as smooth as he ever had in his 9 NBA seasons. The Lakers trailed the Pistons 52–47 at the half, but then the Lakers came out with a 37-point third quarter; 20 of those points came off the fast break. The Lakers went from 5 down to an 83–73 lead after the period, and they hung on to win 108–105.

This was the L.A. break at its best: Kareem on the rebound, then a quick outlet pass to Magic, who had to choose from a variety of wing men to dish off to on the break. He went around his back, behind his head, and every which way to get the ball to Worthy or Green or Byron Scott for another lay-up. One time he even faked the lay-up and dished out to Michael Cooper, who hit a 3-point shot. This was also Earvin at his best.

The half started with a bang for L.A. Actually, that was the sound of a badly missed shot from 3-point range by Isiah Thomas. Magic hauled in the long rebound, and in one continuous move whirled and threw a hook pass way downcourt to Scott, who streaked by the Detroit defense for a slam. When the Pistons came back the other way on a break, Johnson raced back and picked off a pass by Isiah. Magic was at full speed now. He took the pass back downcourt, and threw an over-the-head lead pass to Worthy for another dunk. Score: 54–53.

The rest of the Lakers picked up on Magic's pace when he went to the defensive boards and took a rebound right out of Adrian Dantley's hands, leaving the Piston forward stunned. Suddenly, Kareem was getting down, grabbing his shorts, and playing some tenacious defense on Isiah, of all people. The rest of the Pistons were left stunned.

Kareem then pulled down a board and started the

aforementioned break to put the Lakers ahead for good. Worthy took a long board next and went out on the run. When he hit midcourt, Magic was right there with him. Worthy gave the ball to Magic, who gave it back to Worthy, and he drained the rock. Timeout for the Pistons; this last one had to be seen again. As the instant replay repeated the moment and isolated Magic, Billy Cunningham, commenting for the NBA on CBS, confirmed, ''There is nobody better at playing the middle of the break in the history of the game than Magic Johnson.'' Fade to commercial, with Randy Newman singing ''I Love L.A.'' in the background.

The timeout didn't slow down the Lakers. In a momentary half-court situation, Magic even made quick work of things by feeding Kareem with a low-post pass, then cutting to the hoop for a return pass and a lay-up. The Lakers had hit 6 of 6 shots from the field with 7:30 left in the third quarter (all 6 were lay-ups). And all 6 came off one type of break or another. Magic was even quicker then the Pistons on defense. He beat Dantley to the base line on a drive and drew an offensive foul. Earvin scampered downcourt and dropped off a pass to Kareem, who hit a sky hook to finish off a 16–3 Laker run.

When the break was into high gear, the team was getting nothing but ''easy'' shots. The best way to tell if the break was in stride—besides Magic's smile—was to check the shooting percentages. The Lakers hit their first 9 shots in this quarter and finished the period shooting 74% from the floor.

Only the names changed as Magic continued to run, gun, and have fun. Mychal Thompson checked in for

Kareem just in time to get a quick silver, over-the-head pass from magic standing at the top of the key and convert it for a lay-up. Another Piston missed a shot, and Magic was off and running again. He went to Thompson on the right, and the ball bounced off the head of the Pistons' Joe Dumars into Thompson's hands for a lay-up. When the break was at its best, Magic had everything bouncing his way. He picked up a loose ball at midcourt and had a pass inside deflected to the right wing, where he picked it up and threw a one-hand pass to Thompson cutting to the hole for a bucket. Earvin finally got a breather with 1:29 left in the quarter and the Lakers leading 74–64. But he wasn't finished yet. Cooper hit a 3-point shot to give the team an 83–73 lead going into the fourth, and as soon as the ball went in the net Magic jumped off the bench and celebrated. He hit the Pistons with one more run to start the fourth quarter and then the Lakers coasted to their victory.

To coach Pat Riley this third quarter was a welcome sight. He was near the breaking point at halftime, so he made sure Magic knew how to get the Lakers off and running. "We just talked about being precise and efficient," said the coach. "The rest was all Magic."

Pistons' coach Chuck Daly had another point of view about what had just transpired. "They came out in the third quarter and seized the game. They get a thirty-seven-point quarter and it's lights out. I'm telling my guys, 'Watch out, it may get worse.' It's a credit to them. They're a great basketball team."

Magic had been this way before, where a trail of the opposition's broken hearts, broken dreams, and broken backs lay in his victory wake. But this was a sign of how efficient the Lakers were with Magic leading them on the fast break. Afterwards, as Earvin stood with Brent Musburger and explained to everyone watching on television how he felt, he looked to his left and then he looked to his right. then he cracked a smile. This was the stuff of which highlight films are made.

12

A Final Toast

NORM HUNG UP THE TELEPHONE AND WALKED BACK TO THE bar, laughing. "Oooh, Cliffee, I was just talking on the Larry Bird Line. Utah Jazz Coach Frank Layden—you know the guy who looks like Santa Claus in a sports coat—he wouldn't let anyone else get a word in. He was talking in one-liners, had everybody screaming."

"Yeah, Nahmie—that guy's pretty funny. They say he's the George Wendt of the NBA."

"Yeah, well, see he was talking about Larry Bird and comparing him to Magic Johnson. Seems like everyone's caught up in this conflict over who was better—Magic or good old Lar-Bird."

"Yeah, Nahmie, how about Larry Bird?"

"Anyway, Layden was talking about how the Lakers barely beat his Utah Jazz team in the playoffs last month. He was saying how Karl Malone was talking to the press afterwards about Magic. He was saying how because he's six-foot-nine, he is able to manhandle point guards who have to play him. According to Layden, Malone said, 'Magic Johnson is a very, very good player. But if he were six-foot-two, he'd be just another good guy.' "

"Nahmie, I like that guy Malone. They call him the 'Mailman,' don't they?"

"Hey you, over there in the sunglasses and the flowered shirt—want to borrow fifty cents so you call the Larry Bird Line?"

"Sorry, babe," Jack shot back. "Wrong number. I'm not going to even bother with this question of who's better, Larry Bird or Magic Johnson. It's a real no contest, you know, just like when the Lakers play the Celtics. . . ."

How about a few closing arguments when it comes to the everlasting squabble over who was the better basketball player: Larry Johnson or Magic Bird. The important concept to keep in mind here is that it's about a player, anyone who can walk onto a court in any gymnasium and play his game while everyone watching from the sidelines says, "Now *that's* a player."

The great thing about basketball is that everybody is entitled to his or her own opinion. The great thing about Magic Johnson and Larry Bird is that they were forever changing everybody's opinion.

What would this issue be without a few more numbers to figure? Since Bird and Johnson came into the league, the Lakers and Celtics have played each other 48 times through the 1988–89 season, including the playoffs. The Lakers have won 30 of those games, and as Magic and Larry have each made it known again and again, when you get right down to it the game is all about winning. Make no mistake—with these 2 guys, how they played the game had a direct impact on winning.

In those games, Magic averaged 20.9 points, 7.1 rebounds, and 12.1 assists per game. Bird hit for 24.8 points, 6.6 assists, and 11 rebounds per contest. Overall, Larry had a higher career scoring average, but over the long haul he took more shots. Earvin handled the ball more so he had a better assists average, but he also had more turnovers. Magic was the better career shooter percentage-wise by a few points, but when you get into degree of difficulty, no one could match Larry Bird. Rumor had it that Johnson's position was more demanding because he had to handle the ball so much and take it into the middle of heavy defensive traffic to play his game. But Bird was always, always double-teamed, and usually had more than 2 guys hanging on his jersey as he went to the basket.

If we're talking in terms of winning, which is the way both Bird and Johnson liked to talk, then it gets even more interesting. In his first 9 years, Magic led the Lakers to 5 NBA titles, including the first back-to-back championships in 19 years, and the team played in the NBA championship series in 7 of those 9 years. Magic was the playoff MVP 3 times—1980, 1982, 1987—which made him a true clutch player. The Celtics made it to the NBA Finals 5 times in Bird's first 9 years, and the team won titles in 1981, 1984, and 1986. He was the playoff MVP in the latter 2 series; he was a true clutch player. On the bottom line, the Lakers and Celtics squared off for 3 NBA titles those first 9 years for Larry and Earvin, and the Lakers won twice.

"Comparisons don't mean nothing to me," said Bird.

Kareem Abdul-Jabbar, the elder statesmen of the NBA, became involved in this argument once in a while. But the big guy refused to make the ultimate comparison. "They each give the crowd so much to enjoy, whether they win or not," he said. "Their effort and intensity make fans enjoy watching the type of plays they make. People who don't really know the game of basketball from a technical viewpoint can watch Magic or Bird and begin to appreciate what the sport is all about."

After 9 years in the game, Bird and Johnson still managed to sustain their enthusiasm for the game—and kept it at the level they had when they first came into the league. Something made them the *ultimate* players. They went out with the same do-or-die, helter-skelter, don't-give-up intensity through each game of the 1988 season.

"I still don't get tired during a game," said Bird. "I still want to play forty-eight minutes every night." Added Magic: "I just love to play the game, just be out there. When I am, I'm in my own little world."

The only way to settle this argument is to realize that the game wouldn't be the same without Larry Bird and Magic Johnson playing together, pushing each other to be the best.

"He elevates me," said the Magic Man. "It is special to play Larry Bird. It's fun; it's exciting. It's not a personal thing between us. One time we did a commercial together and we found out we had a lot in common. We found out we really enjoyed each other. Larry and I motivate each other. He was the motivation for me when I won my MVP, and I know I motivated him to get it back. He always wants to come back and prove he's the best. It would be a different game if he was gone. He's my measuring stick.''

Perhaps their true impact on basketball could only be measured during the 1989 NBA All-Star Weekend in Houston. During the previous 9 years the league's annual circus of the stars had more or less been a showcase for Magic and the Bird.

All-Star Saturday—the day before the game—always featured Larry spotting up for the AT&T Long Distance Shootout and challenging the rest of the best in the league to prove he wasn't the deadliest 3-point marksman in the game. All-Star Sunday—game day—was Magic's opportunity to get out on the break and dazzle the crowd with no–look passes to Karl Malone and Akeem Olajuwon filling the lanes. This was the time of the year when Earvin and Larry always delivered.

But something was obviously missing from the 1989 extravaganza.

On November 18, 1988 Larry Bird underwent surgery to remove 2 small bone spurs embedded in the Achilles tendon of each of his feet. At the time the prognosis after a successful operation was that the Bird Man would return to active playing duty by the beginning of March, 1989. At the beginning of March, though, Bird admitted he was nowhere near ready to play, and the Celtics speculated that he may not return for the remainder of the season.

Late in January of 1989, Magic Johnson was making a move to the basket when he suffered a partial tear of his left hamstring. The Magic Man had been having another MVP season, complete with such heroics as a half-court 3-point shot as the final buzzer sounded to beat the Detroit Pistons in December of 1988. Such a

shot prompted the folks at the NBA office to make a
new promotional commercial, including that magic moment. In his tenth season, Earvin was proving that he
was better than ever.

But as the All-Star Weekend of 1989 headed into full
swing, Magic was lounging by the pool at his Bel Air
mansion and Larry was back in Boston rehabilitating his
healing Achilles. The pre-game television show on CBS
was more like a big get-well card as each of the NBA
stars took the opportunity to wish both Magic and the
Bird the best. Kareem grabbed the microphone from
CBS announcer Pat O'Brien and said, "Get well soon,
Magic. I miss you already." Added Detroit's Isiah
Thomas: "It just isn't the same without Magic and
Larry."

The show went on, but it wasn't the same—for the
players or the ratings. In fact, the national telecast of
the Indiana University–University of Michigan college
game drew more of an audience that afternoon of February 12.

But perhaps such an absence only served to prolong
the magic. Prior to his surgery, Bird had said he was in
pain just standing. As 2 bone spurs were removed from
one heel, and one from the other in a 90–minute operation at New England Baptist Hospital, Bird maintained
his usual good spirits. What would he do to fill up all
the time normally overloaded with basketball that season? "Maybe I'll take up roofing," he quipped.

Both of Bird's surgens—team doctor Arnold Scheller
and Roger Mann, a foot specialist from San Francisco—
pronounced the surgery "very successful." Such would
seem to be enough reason to believe Bird would return
to his rare form, but any remaining doubt must have

been removed when he signed a new contract to take him through the 1991–92 season. The deal netted Bird $1.8 million in 1988–89 and $4.2 million during the course of the following 2 seasons.

No worries about Magic, either. He returned to his old form after sitting out 2 weeks to heal his hamstring and in another week he was back among the league leaders in assists and scoring. The Lakers, as usual, were high atop the Pacific division and the NBA's Western Conference, where they remained for the rest of the season.

At the time of his injury, Magic hinted that he may have 2 good years left in him. "I'll still be young then," he said, but mind- and body-wise I'll be an old man." That would make his final season the 1991–92 campaign.

And that is just too accurate for irony. It was no small coincidence that Magic and Bird came into the league at the same time, and it was no great surprise that they planned to make a grand exit together. "Got to go out on top," said Bird.

If there is any justice in life, Magic and Bird will meet for the NBA championship in 1991 or 1992, and the Celtics will beat the Lakers in triple overtime of the seventh game when Bird beats the final buzzer with a shot from just inside the half-court line. Left-handed. Or how about a final flurry in the Garden, when Magic drives on Bird, and throws in a running-hook shot as he falls to the floor. Left-handed.

Finally, we can get the last word on this question of who is better, Magic or the Bird.

"You know, Sam," Nahmie started. "I think I've seen enough of this Johnson guy. I wouldn't even put him on the all-Johnson team."

"Now hold on there a minute, Nahmie. If you and me and Sam and everyone else, if we're true basketball fans, maybe we have to take another look here. We have a saying down there at the U.S. Postal Service: Don't lick the envelope before you put the letter in. It will leave a bad taste in your mouth. This here Magic Man; we put him in the same class with good old Lar-Bird, and it just puts them up there on the pedestal as the two greatest players in the game. And let's face it, when you get right down to it, Larry Bird and Magic Johnson can only be compared to each other. It's kind of like if Marilyn Monroe and Raquel Welch lived across the street from each other. . . ."

"No, not that one again, Cliffee. But I think you just may have something there, buddy. Sam, give me another round. Everybody raise their glasses and join me in this one final toast."

To Magic and the Bird, we say: *"Cheers."*